CONTENTS

NEW DIRECTIONS FOR STUDENT SERVICES

John H. Schuh, *Iowa State University*
EDITOR-IN-CHIEF

Elizabeth J. Whitt, *University of Iowa*
ASSOCIATE EDITOR

The Implications of Student Spirituality for Student Affairs Practice

Margaret A. Jablonski
Brown University

EDITOR

Number 95, Fall 2001

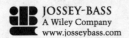
JOSSEY-BASS
A Wiley Company
www.josseybass.com

THE IMPLICATIONS OF STUDENT SPIRITUALITY FOR STUDENT AFFAIRS PRACTICE
Margaret A. Jablonski (ed.)
New Directions for Student Services, no. 95
John H. Schuh, Editor-in-Chief
Elizabeth J. Whitt, Associate Editor

Microfilm copies of issues and articles are available in 16mm and 35mm, as well as microfiche in 105mm, through University Microfilms Inc., 300 North Zeeb Road, Ann Arbor, Michigan 48106-1346.

ISSN 0164-7970   ISBN 0-7879-5787-9

NEW DIRECTIONS FOR STUDENT SERVICES is part of The Jossey-Bass Higher and Adult Education Series and is published quarterly by Jossey-Bass, 989 Market Street, San Francisco, California 94103-1741. Periodicals postage paid at San Francisco, California, and at additional mailing offices. Postmaster: Send address changes to New Directions for Student Services, Jossey-Bass, 989 Market Street, San Francisco, California 94103-1741.

New Directions for Student Services is indexed in College Student Personnel Abstracts and Contents Pages in Education.

SUBSCRIPTIONS cost $59.00 for individuals and $114.00 for institutions, agencies, and libraries. See ordering information page at end of book.

EDITORIAL CORRESPONDENCE should be sent to the Editor-in-Chief, John H. Schuh, N 243 Lagomarcino Hall, Iowa State University, Ames, Iowa 50011

Cover photograph by Wernher Krutein/PHOTOVAULT © 1990.

Jossey-Bass Web address: www.josseybass.com

EDITOR'S NOTES

Why publish an issue on spirituality and campus life? Student affairs and student affairs preparation programs have been reluctant to address spirituality as connected to student development or to the programs and services on a college campus. This volume of *New Directions for Student Services* offers student affairs professionals and others on college campuses information and guidance about including spirituality in student life programs, and in the curriculum of professional preparation programs for student affairs. As Love and Talbot argue, "student affairs professionals must understand the role that such values as faith, hope, and love play in the structure and persistence of communities, in the construction of knowledge, in the understanding of truth, and in developmental processes of students" (1999).

For the purposes of this volume, we use the two terms *spirituality* and *religion*. Each chapter makes a distinction between the two terms clear in its discussion. In general, for us to have some common language, we use *spiritual development* in the context that Love and Talbot (1999) do. They describe five interrelated processes that incorporate various belief systems and traditional religions:

1. Spiritual development involves an internal process of seeking personal authenticity, genuineness, and wholeness as an aspect of identity development.
2. Spiritual development involves the process of continually transcending one's current locus of centricity.
3. Spiritual development involves developing a greater connectedness to self and others through relationships and union with community.
4. Spiritual development involves deriving meaning, purpose, and direction in one's life.
5. Spiritual development involves increasing openness to exploring a relationship with an intangible and pervasive power or essence that exists beyond human existence and rational human knowing (p. 364).

Over the past two hundred years, public higher education traditionally has maintained a separation of church and state. From the historical context, an economic purpose of education was to provide practical knowledge to succeed in life. By the end of the nineteenth century, religion had largely disappeared from public schools. Although most public and private colleges were founded in conjunction with a particular denomination (mostly

Preparation of this issue was made possible with the assistance of Sally Sundquist, at the University of Connecticut; and Vachel Miller, at the University of Massachusetts, Amherst.

1

Protestant, Catholic, and recently some Jewish), in the past century there was a marked move away from the trappings of organized religion on the college campus. For example, mandatory chapel and the senior capstone course on morality or philosophy were eliminated. In the twentieth century, modern science took center stage, featuring research that created new ways of understanding life, organizations, and human nature. No longer was religion needed to explain the nature or order of the world.

The U.S. Supreme Court has said that public education must be neutral in matters of religion (not favoring one religion over another), but neither can it favor nonreligion over religion. In the 1947 *Everson* ruling, Justice Hugo Black said that "state power is no more to be used so as to handicap religions than it is to favor them." Similarly, in *Abington* v. *Schempp* (1963) Justice Tom C. Clark wrote in the majority opinion that public schools cannot favor "those who believe in no religion over those who do believe."

However, there has been an emphasis on neutrality, which has led to marginalization or exclusion. Alan Wolfe, a leading scholar on religion and higher education, says: "today we risk a different kind of homogenization—we have become so secular that we leave little room for religious expression. If anything, the secular version of the university has been such a success that its way of doing business constitutes a new orthodoxy" (1997, p. B4).

The 1960s and 1970s saw students who were antiestablishment and therefore not interested in, or openly hostile to, religion. Many explored alternative forms of spirituality, seeking personal growth and enrichment from meditation, Buddhism, or nature-based religions. The 1980s brought the pursuit of materialism as the central value for many students. In the last decade, however, there has been resurgence in spiritual exploration and religion. Go into any bookstore and check the best-seller listings; you will find numerous books published in the past few years with *spirit, soul,* and even *spiritual intelligence* in the title. Then find the sections on religion and spirituality (usually combined), and you will see hundreds of books written in the past decade that focus on the meaning of life, human nature, relationships, and so on, all from a spiritual perspective. (See the Annotated References chapter at the end of this volume.) In the presidential race of 2000, the two major-party candidates proclaimed themselves born-again Christians; there was also a vice presidential candidate who practiced and spoke about his Jewish faith.

The influence of spirituality has been seen in the curriculum of some departments of education, sociology, psychology, and business, particularly at the graduate level. Parker Palmer has written extensively (1993, 1998, 1998–99) about teaching and learning from the inside out, with spirituality being central to learning. His works are cited regularly in education courses. Ken Blanchard, the "one-minute manager" guru of management seminars, recently turned to infusing values, principles, and beliefs into leadership and the organization. Margaret Wheatley also explored leadership and spirituality (1992) and principles of organizational development as connected to both science and spirituality (1996).

Today, many students are coming to college as believers in some faith; participating in practices such as community service, meditation, or yoga; and seeking answers to questions about purpose, mission, and values. A liberal education offers exposure to various traditions, ways of thinking, and practices. As we are beginning to add the spiritual perspective to a number of fields of inquiry and outside of classroom experience, we student affairs professionals need to become more inclusive of spirituality in all the programs and services we offer.

This also is connected to multiculturalism, looking at issues of education and society from various perspectives: race, ethnicity, gender, sexual orientation, and so on. Weaving multicultural voices into the curriculum and cocurriculum proved controversial, but it is now commonplace to consider multiple perspectives on any subject. The next step involves drawing diverse spiritual voices (which may include religious voices) into the multicultural paradigm.

Student affairs embodies many principles of a liberal education, including education of the whole person. In one of the original founding documents of the profession, the *Student Personnel Point of View* (American Council on Education, 1937), spiritual development was explicitly included with occupational, intellectual, and other forms of human development. Many of our models of student development theory (Chickering and Reisser, 1993; Baxter Magolda, 1992) also address issues of values, morals, and ethical development. Although those models do not explicitly connect spirituality to student development, if their authors were writing today they might use this more inclusive term. Over the past decade, reviews of student affairs programs have emphasized creating purposeful models that address growth and development of students from a holistic perspective (Blimling and Whitt, 1999; Kuh, Schuh, and Whitt, 1991). Many of our student life programs use a wellness model for program design that includes a spiritual dimension.

Chapter Summaries

This volume groups together chapters that relate to particular aspects of student affairs: students (both undergraduates and those in preparation programs), organizational life, theory and practice of leadership and staff development, and resources for continued exploration.

In Chapter One, Patrick Love examines student development theory and the place of spiritual development within them. He considers the work of Sharon Parks (1986, 2000) as the centerpiece upon which his chapter is grounded. Parks emphasizes the interrelatedness of cognitive development with social and cultural influences, including religion and spiritual growth. Love explores forms of knowing, dependence, and community from adolescence through young adulthood. He offers several implications for student affairs practice, among them creation of mentoring communities and other student life programs that explicitly address spiritual development.

In Chapter Two, Jon Dalton looks at how students explore questions of purpose and truth. He describes the searching that ultimately makes a connection with one's life purpose—a calling or a career. He describes students as engaged with ethical and spiritual questions through community service, campus leadership, and other pursuits. Dalton encourages other student life professionals to create structured opportunities for students to examine spiritual aspects of the big questions: commitment, responsibility, and moral decision.

In Chapter Three, Kathleen Manning discusses recent developments concerning the infusion of soul into the workplace, including college campus environments. She refers to popular writers such as Bolman and Deal (1995) in considering issues of spirituality in organizational theory and student affairs practice. Manning outlines where in student affairs administration soul and spirit are emerging: student leadership, service learning, campus traditions, and orientation programs.

In Chapter Four, Tom Clark outlines the particular challenges student affairs professionals face in dealing with spiritual life on the college campus. He gives an overview of how higher education became secularized, with neutrality leading to marginalization of anything resembling organized religion. He offers some advice for student affairs staff to enable discussion of spiritual issues on all campuses, public and private.

In Chapter Five, Kathleen Allen and Gar Kellom share with us their perspectives on leadership, staff development, and organizational design to incorporate aspects of spirit into student affairs. They write from years of experience leading staff development programs and trying new ways of managing and leading staff. They offer suggestions for creating an organization that supports spiritual work: changing the environment, designing reasonable jobs, and shifting criteria for performance evaluation. They have several practical suggestions for staff development activities for the student affairs staff.

In Chapter Six, Carney Strange examines preparing graduate students to serve in the field of student affairs. Strange proposes that we consider curricular and outside-of-classroom experiences that give students the opportunity to explore their learning in a spiritual context. He discusses how students make meaning of their experiences and the need to create an environment that supports exploration of spiritual questions. He suggests that student affairs preparation programs include rite and ritual, to connect students to one another and the institution. His chapter offers practical examples for exploring differences, mentoring students, examining the big questions, and dealing with other aspects of graduate education.

In Chapter Seven, Alicia Fedelina Chávez explores a scholar-practitioner's perspective on incorporating spiritual principles into everyday student affairs practice. Writing from a Native American and Spanish Catholic heritage, Chávez outlines ten guiding principles for her life, which she connects with her roles as a college administrator and faculty member.

She discusses her struggle to embody compassion, maintain connectedness, live a life of purposeful reflection, hold relationship sacred, steward, live simply and in balance, radiate hopefulness, and give thanks within a higher education context. She discusses how to live in congruence with one's spiritual and philosophical worldview while developing the ability to work across differences in a multicultural community.

In Chapter Eight, Shirley Williams gives the reader numerous resources for further exploration of spirit at work and in education; books, articles, Websites, conferences, retreat centers, and other resources are identified briefly. Although not comprehensive, the list of resources covers a variety of perspectives and traditions.

Margaret A. Jablonski
Editor

References

Abington v. Schempp, 374 U.S. 203, 225, 83 S. Ct. 1560, 1573 (1963).

American Council on Education. *The Student Personnel Point of View.* (American Council on Education Studies, series 1, no. 3.) Washington, D.C.: American Council on Education, 1937.

Baxter Magolda, M. *Knowing and Reasoning in College: Gender-Related Patterns in Students' Intellectual Development.* San Francisco: Jossey-Bass, 1992.

Blimling, G., and Whitt, E. *Good Practices in Student Affairs: Principles to Foster Student Learning.* San Francisco: Jossey-Bass, 1999.

Bolman, L. G., and Deal T. E. *Leading with Soul: An Uncommon Journey of Spirit.* San Francisco: Jossey-Bass, 1995.

Chickering, A. and Reisser, L. *Education and Identity.* (2nd ed.) San Francisco: Jossey-Bass, 1993.

Kuh, G., Schuh, J., and Whitt, E. *Involving Colleges: Encouraging Student Learning and Personal Development Through Out-of-Classroom Experiences.* San Francisco: Jossey-Bass, 1991.

Love, P., and Talbot, D. "Defining Spiritual Development: A Missing Consideration for Student Affairs." *NASAP Journal,* 1999, 37, 361–375.

Palmer, P. *To Know As We Are Known: Education As a Spiritual Journey.* San Francisco: Harper San Francisco, 1993.

Palmer, P. *The Courage to Teach: Exploring the Inner Landscape of a Teacher's Life.* San Francisco: Jossey-Bass, 1998.

Palmer, P. "Evoking the Spirit." *Educational Leadership,* Dec. 1998–Jan. 1999, 6–11.

Parks, S. *The Critical Years: Young Adults and the Search for Meaning, Faith, and Commitment.* New York: HarperCollins, 1986.

Parks, S. *Big Questions, Worthy Dreams: Mentoring Young Adults in Their Search for Meaning, Purpose, and Faith.* San Francisco: Jossey-Bass, 2000.

Wheatley, M. *Leadership and the New Science: Learning About Organization from an Orderly Universe.* San Francisco: Berrett-Koehler, 1992.

Wheatley, M. *A Simpler Way.* San Francisco: Berrett-Koehler, 1996.

Wolfe, A. "A Welcome Revival of Religion in the Academy." *The Chronicle of Higher Education,* 1997, 44(4), B4.

MARGARET A. JABLONSKI *is dean for campus life at Brown University. She has worked for more than twenty years in higher education in student affairs and as a faculty member. She is interested in organizational change, leadership, women's issues, and spirituality.*

1

Student Development Theory, the foundation for much of student affairs practice, is examined and expanded upon to include spiritual development.

Spirituality and Student Development: Theoretical Connections

Patrick G. Love

As was pointed out in the Editor's Notes in this volume, there is a surge of interest in the spiritual development of college students. This chapter considers where theories of spiritual development fit into the constellation of student development theories. The centerpiece is the work of Sharon Daloz Parks (1986, 2000). Parks is a theorist whose perspectives are those of someone trained in theology who has worked as a minister and with college students. She grounds her work in both the psychosocial and cognitive/structural traditions of student development theory. She emphasizes the interrelatedness of cognitive development; affective states; and interpersonal, social, and cultural influences.

Parks's original work builds on James Fowler's theory of faith development (1981). She extends Fowler's work by proposing another stage of faith development between adolescent and adult, which she calls "young adult" and which includes traditional-aged college students. She uses and compares her work to the theories and research of Jean Piaget, William Perry, Robert Kegan, Erik Erikson, Lawrence Kohlberg, and Carol Gilligan, so it is grounded in traditional student development theory. In this chapter, Parks's work on faith development is compared primarily to Perry's scheme of intellectual development. Given space considerations, I have chosen Perry's work over that of more recent theorists (for example, Baxter Magolda, 1992; and King and Kitchener, 1994) because their work is built on Perry's foundation.

NEW DIRECTIONS FOR STUDENT SERVICES, no. 95, Fall 2001 © John Wiley & Sons, Inc.

Religion, Spiritual Development, and Faith Development

It is important to differentiate the notion of religion from issues of spirituality and faith, because the terms are often used interchangeably ("What faith are you?" "I'm a Catholic."). Religion is a shared system of beliefs, principles, or doctrines related to a belief in and worship of a supernatural power or powers regarded as creator(s) and governor(s) of the universe. Parks (2000) views spirituality to be a search for meaning, transcendence, wholeness, purpose, and "apprehension of spirit (or Spirit) as the animating essence at the core of life" (p. 16), a search more personal than public. Ideally, religion and spirituality significantly overlap. However, there are religious people tied so closely to dogma and doctrine as to be disconnected from issues of the spirit, and people who disavow any notion of or connection with religion yet are deeply involved in a search for meaning, wholeness, and purpose.

Parks (2000), like Fowler (1981) before her, speaks of faith development as opposed to spiritual development. Faith is a process of meaning making, which is the process of making sense out of the activities of life and seeking patterns, order, coherence, and relation among the disparate elements of human living. It is the process of discovering and creating connections among experiences and events. It is differentiated somewhat from traditional cognitive development theories because it is the activity of seeking and composing meaning involving the most comprehensive dimensions of our experience. Parks describes this notion of faith as both transcendent and immanent. That is, in the experience and activity of faith, it lies beyond the range of ordinary perception and experience and thus is ultimately unknowable, *and* it remains within us and the particulars of our experience.

Parks (2000) describes four interacting levels that compose faith: self, other, world, and "God." Self is the individual meaning maker, other includes the immediate interactions and relationships with those beyond the self, world is the recognition of existence and influence of others beyond one's immediate relationships and interactions, and "God" is the center of power and value for the individual. Parks places the word *God* within quotation marks to differentiate between God as a supreme being and God as an idea— a focus, a center, a cause, something to which the individual is committed. As Parks indicates, a person of faith may well deny the existence of a supernatural being called God, but that individual at least would be living with confidence in some center of value and with loyalty to some cause. These four elements make up the gestalt of one's faith and undergo dynamic change and transformation during the developmental process.

Faith Development and Student Development

Parks (2000) presents a three-component model of faith development. The three interacting components she describes are forms of knowing (cognitive aspects of faith development), forms of dependence (an affective aspect of faith development), and forms of community (social aspects of faith development). The cognitive component is grounded in the work of Perry (1970) and Fowler (1981), and the forms of knowing and their development correspond with the structures posited by Perry, Fowler, and other cognitive-structural theorists. Fowler's theory describes seven stages of faith development that cover the life span. Here, according to Fowler, are the five stages most likely to be experienced by college students:

Examples of Fowler's Stages of Faith Development
- The opportunity to experience great joy from student affairs work
- The sense of accomplishment possible when involved with educating students
- The possibility of career satisfaction that is not solely linked to materialism
- The chance to celebrate students' success and our own
- The pursuit of a lifestyle marked by health and wellness

Parks describes forms of dependence as affective aspects of faith development; they focus on how people feel. However, in discussing the various stages of dependence she also describes interpersonal interactions (which are social aspects of development) and the view of oneself as an authority figure (which is an aspect of cognitive development). She describes the dependence part of her model as focusing on the relationships through which we discover and change our views of knowledge and faith. More than the other two elements of her model, the forms of dependence demonstrate the interactive nature of the components of her model.

Forms of community address a "neglect" (Kegan, 1982) in many cognitive development theories or in the synopses of cognitive development theory, which is the failure to give adequate recognition to the influence of the interpersonal, social, and cultural context on one's development. Piaget (1969) was clear about the influence that interaction with the environment had on cognitive development, but it was a fact often overlooked by those who followed him or sought to extend his theory (Parks, 2000). Parks's model focuses particularly on community because it identifies the tension between the desire for agency and autonomy and the desire for belonging, connection, and intimacy. Taken together, her interacting components of faith development bring together the cognitive, affective, and interpersonal elements of human existence. The addition of the dependence and community components draws somewhat on the work of Erikson (1968), and especially on Kegan (1994), who is the only other major student development theorist proposing a theory that integrates the cognitive, affective, and social aspects of development (Love and Guthrie, 1999).

Parks asserts that most stage-related developmental theories jump directly from adolescent to adult and attribute any "noise" or anomalies between those two stages to the transition from adolescence to adulthood. She argues instead that there is actually another stage of development between adolescence and adulthood, which she labels young adult. She also differentiates in adulthood between tested adults and mature adults. This results in a four-stage model of development: adolescent or conventional, young adult, tested adult, and mature adult.

Adolescent or Conventional. Before students embark on the developmental journey to adulthood, Parks (2000) sees their faith—the meaning they make of the world—existing first in a form that is based in and dependent on authority in the context of a monolithic community that defines "us" (in the community) and "them" (outside the community). During this stage of development, the absolute form of knowing breaks down and other perspectives are heard and recognized, the individual grows in self-awareness, authorities may be resisted, and the definition and experience of the community become more diffuse. This is a time of great ambiguity and uncertainty for individuals in their journey of faith development.

Forms of Knowing. The forms of knowing in the model presented by Parks (2000) reflect the cognitive developmental aspect of faith development. In the adolescent or conventional stage of faith development, the forms of knowing are authority-bound and dualistic and unqualified relativism. Authority-bound and dualistic knowing is grounded in some form of authority that exists outside of oneself. It can be easily recognized as an element within one's life (for example, one's religion, the Bible, the Constitution) or a person or group (parents, teachers, clergy). It also can be more socially pervasive and subtle, as with the unquestioned authority of media, culturally affirmed roles and personalities (experts, artists, entertainers), and customs (conventions of thought, feeling, behavior; Parks, 2000). As individuals experience the breakdown in the absolute nature of authority in their life, they shift to the form of knowing that Parks labeled unqualified relativism. This form of knowing is recognition on the part of the knower that "all knowledge is shaped by, and thus relative to, the context and relationships within which it is composed . . . and every opinion and judgment may be as worthy as any other" (p. 57).

Like Parks, Perry (1970) labeled the first position in his scheme of intellectual development dualism. However, from her description of the unqualified-relativism form of knowing, Parks (2000) appears to have collapsed the distinction between Perry's positions of multiplicity and relativism. This lack of differentiation becomes evident because her next form of knowing (probing commitment) is related more closely to Perry's position of initial commitment in relativism. Perry differentiated multiplicity and relativism because of their distinctive set of underlying assumptions. Although recognizing the existence of ambiguity and uncertainty, Perry (1970) described multiplicity as still being grounded in the basic assumptions of dualism—that ultimately there is one truth, one right answer to all questions, and the hope that the world is ultimately knowable. Relativism, on the other hand, is grounded in different assumptions: acceptance that the world is inherently ambiguous, complex, and unknowable.

Forms of Dependence. The adolescent or conventional forms of dependence are dependent and counterdependent. By dependence, Parks (2000) means that "a person's sense of self and truth depends upon his or her immediate relational and affectional ties in a primary way" (p. 74). One's form of knowing during this time is especially *dependent* on whatever and whoever the authority is in one's life. Other cognitive development theorists (Baxter Magolda, 1992; Belenky, Clinchy, Goldberger, and Tarule, 1986; and King and Kitchener, 1994) either directly or indirectly described the dependence of authority-bound knowers. Belenky, Clinchy, Goldberger, and Tarule (1986) describe a particularly pernicious form of dependence in their "silence" status, where women had no voice and little sense of self.

Counterdependence is movement in opposition to authority. Parks (2000) indicates that this is an aspect of the adolescent stage, without indicating that it follows directly from dependence or necessarily has to occur at all. The individual is moving away from or against the authority she or he knows, rather than actively moving toward a new authority or new truth. The adolescent is still dependent on the former truth because, absent a new truth, what they know to be true is *not* what they formerly held to be true: "I don't know what I want (or believe), but I know it isn't this."

Forms of Community. Parks (2000) identifies two forms of community that take place during a person's journey through the adolescent stage of faith development: conventional and diffuse. A conventional community is one in which conformity by members to cultural norms, interests, and assumptions is expected and enforced. It is homogeneous in that the core expectation is that the community is made up of people who are "like us." Just as absolute authority and dependence on a single authority eventually break down, the monolithic nature of the community breaks down as well, or at least a person's willingness to define self solely as a member of one particular community declines. Just as in multiplicity each opinion or truth claim is granted equivalent status (Perry, 1970), so are relationships as one enters the diffuse stage of development. One becomes more open to expanding the notion of community, but one's commitment to any particular community weakens.

Summary of Adolescent/Conventional. How one makes sense of the world, and how one answers the ultimate questions we face as sentient beings (such as Why am I here?) during adolescence, usually begins with simple answers representing a simple view of a straightforward and knowable world. There are answers to our questions, and they reside in the authorities in our lives; the answers are shared among those in our community. Along the way, this innocent view of the world comes under stress. Authorities are found to be in error, undependable, or in conflict. Communities other than that which supports a conventional view are experienced and discovered to have some validity or worth. These experiences can result in loss of faith, though it is a loss of naïve faith, and a loss that actually signals a developmental movement forward. We then embark upon the most significant transition of faith development, that stage Parks has labeled young adult.

Young Adult. Because of cultural changes during the last century, Parks argues that it is time to consider another distinguishable phase between adolescence and full adulthood, which she has labeled young adult. Parks (2000) indicates that most developmental psychologists do not recognize such a stage; instead, they refer to it as the process of transition between adolescence and full adulthood. For example, in their synthesis of cognitive development theories, Love and Guthrie (1999) identify "the great accommodation." This is the accommodation of cognitive structures where a person transitions from seeing the world as ultimately knowable and certain to seeing the world as complex, ambiguous, and not completely knowable. It is also the time when the individual's own role as knower and authority emerges. They locate this great transitional phase at about the place where Parks has added the young adult stage.

Forms of Knowing. Parks (2000) labels the form of knowing in this stage probing commitment. One who is at the young adult stage recognizes that in the complex and contextual nature of the world there is the necessity to take action, choose a path, shape one's own future. One constructs a faith; one constructs meaning. She adds probing commitment between Fowler's third stage (synthetic-conventional) and his fourth stage (individuative-reflective) of faith development (1981). In the synthetic-conventional stage, an individual is developing an integrated identity, but it is based on tacit elements of the culture in which the individual is embedded. There is then a leap to the individuative-reflective stage, where one becomes able to critically choose one's beliefs, values, and commitments. Parks argues that there is a stage in between where an individual makes and learns from tentative commitments. This stage corresponds closely to Perry's position of initial commitment in relativism (1970).

Forms of Dependence. Parks (2000) describes the form of dependence at the young adult stage as fragile inner-dependence. By fragile she does not mean weak, feeble, or puny. Instead, she uses the term as someone would describe a sapling: vulnerable, but healthy, vital, and full of promise. Parks compares this emerging sense of self-authority to the notion of subjective knowing where trust in one's own knowledge and experience is recognized (Belenky, Clinchy, Golberger, and Tarule, 1986). In our complex modern society, there is a slow and sporadic transition from full dependence upon parents or authorities to independence and autonomy. One can recognize the ability to shape one's future and make decisions, while recognizing, for example, the financial resources received from parents that allow continuation of school.

Forms of Community. Parks (2000) labels the form of community needed by a young adult to help with developing a complex adult faith as a mentoring community. She argues that a critical, cognitive self-aware perspective on one's familiar value orientation alone or with a single mentoring figure is not enough to precipitate a transformation in faith. The growth that comes with critical self-awareness must be grounded in the experience of a compatible social group, what she terms a mentoring community. It "offers a network of belonging in which young adults feel recognized as who they really are, and as who they are becoming. It offers both challenge and support and thus offers good company for both the emerging strength and the distinctive vulnerability of the young adult" (2000, p. 95). Although Parks cites the residence hall as a potential mentoring community, her description of this type of community more readily brings to mind the proliferating learning community or living-learning center. It also appears that the culture forming potential mentoring communities needs to be considered. The stronger the culture, the less one is able to deviate from the norms, and the less one is able to tentatively probe a commitment.

Summary of Young Adult. Young adult is the stage at which most traditional-age college students find themselves. In the process of faith development, students new to college may experience "functional regression" (Love and Guthrie, 1999), where by undertaking new learning in a new environment they appropriately regress to previous, more comfortable stages until they feel comfortable in the new environment. Upon entering college, students may regress to authority-bound truth as provided by professors or administrators, return to greater dependence on others in authority, and experience college as a diffuse and confusing set of communities; or latch on to a single, authoritarian community (a cult being a most extreme example). College is also a time when initial probing commitments are made and remade, when the emerging sense of inner-dependence is tested, and when there is opportunity to experience one or more mentoring communities.

Tested Adult and Mature Adult. Parks (2000) describes the development that occurs beyond the young adult stage. Those individuals who reach the tested adult stage may very well be undergraduates, but they are more likely to be postgraduates, graduate students, or beyond. Parks argues that a mature adult faith rarely is in evidence before midlife.

Forms of Knowing. Parks (2000) does not describe the stages of tested commitment and convictional commitment in much depth. As she indicates with tested commitment, "one's form of knowing and being takes on a tested quality, a sense of fittingness, a recognition that one is willing to make one's peace and to affirm one's place in the scheme of things" (p. 69). There is a reduction in the ambiguity and dividedness that marked the early period of probing commitment. Perry's focus on commitment in relativism (positions 6–9 of his scheme) were the least developed aspects of his theory (Love and Guthrie, 1999). In a way, Parks (2000) suffers from the same drawback in her model (though it must be stated that the focus of her work is on young adults).

Forms of Dependence. In the last two stages of Parks's model (2000), the individual moves from a fragile inner-dependence to a confident inner-dependence and then to interdependence. The movement in faith development she describes is from an external focus (dependence on an external authority) to an internal focus (inner-dependence), to an interaction and healthy integration of the two, and to recognition that throughout one's life there has existed interdependence.

Forms of Community. Finally, there are the forms of community in which the individual developing in faith finds oneself. At the tested adult stage, the tendency is to feel most comfortable in a self-selected class or group. This tends to be a group that shares the meanings of the tested adult, with similar socioeconomic, political, religious, and philosophical views. Parks then describes the movement of the individual seeking participation in communities that are open to and seeking others who hold different views and perspectives from one's own. This is similar to Fowler's stage of conjunctive faith (1981), where there is genuine openness to truths, traditions, and communities other than one's own. It is a disciplined openness to the truth of those who are "other."

Summary of Tested Adult and Mature Adult. The movement toward a mature adult faith is one of connection to, interaction with, and belonging to the broader world. It involves recognition of one's interdependence and interconnectedness with communities and individuals beyond one's perceptual scope. It involves growing comfortable with and actually welcoming the ambiguity and doubt that exists even within tested convictions.

Implications for Student Affairs Professionals

Student affairs professionals need to reflect on their own spiritual development. If spirituality and spiritual development are inherent in all people (and not just "religious" people), then we need to consider this developmental process in our own lives. This means considering how we create meaning, purpose, and direction in our lives, the forms of dependence that exist in our relationships, and the types of community to which we belong. This can be done in a variety of ways: during staff training, by using staff meetings differently, through critical reflection and journaling, and so on.

Spiritual Development and Religious Practice. We need to recognize the spiritual aspects of everyday life and not just associate spirituality with religious practice. Students' involvement in social, volunteer, leadership, and community service activity may be a manifestation of their spiritual development and quest for meaning. We also need to recognize that religious activity and other spiritually related activities may be manifestations of students' search for meaning and faith.

Further Considerations of Student Development. Focusing on enhancement of students' cognitive and psychosocial development will in all likelihood contribute to their spiritual development. The close relationship between faith development and other student development theories, especially cognitive development theory, allows student affairs staff to create experiences, activities, and environments that enhance overall growth, as well as spiritual development. For example, many student judicial systems encourage students to reflect on their actions and how those actions affect others and the community. In this way, the student is encouraged to consider his or her form of knowing, form of dependence, and form of community.

Mentoring Communities. Create mentoring communities and review current student groups and organizations as potential mentoring communities; address communities that are contrary to the notion of a mentoring community. Parks describes the potential of communities to greatly influence the spiritual development of students. In addition to trying to create such communities on campus, student affairs professionals should assess already existing groups to see in what ways they can be encouraged to become mentoring communities. Finally, be aware of and address the activities of communities where unreflective commitment is demanded. One need only think of the unhealthy aspects of the pledging experience of fraternities and sororities, organizations with powerful cultures.

Spiritual Development in Graduate Education. Explore inclusion of spiritual development in higher education master's and doctoral programs. Incorporating faith and spiritual development into courses on student development is an additional means of legitimizing this work; it better prepares student affairs professionals to recognize elements of spiritual development in the experiences of their students.

Importance of Spiritual Development. Explicitly state that spiritual development is important for college students. We need to bring spirituality into education, not keep it separate and banished to small sectors of campus (the religious studies department, the campus ministry). The U.S. Constitution states that we may not favor one religion over another—not that we must totally erase all notions of spiritual development from public life and the academy.

Conclusion

The work of Sharon Daloz Parks (2000) reinforces the relationship of spiritually related developmental theories and traditional ones, especially the cognitive-structural. Both sets of theories focus on how people make meaning of the world they live in and the experiences they have. Student affairs staff need to explore faith development theory and the implications that stem from it for students on their campuses.

References

Baxter Magolda, M. B. *Knowing and Reasoning in College: Gender-Related Patterns in Students' Intellectual Development.* San Francisco: Jossey-Bass, 1992.

Belenky, M., Clinchy, B., Goldberger, N., and Tarule, J. *Women's Ways of Knowing: The Development of Self, Voice, and Mind.* New York: Basic Books, 1986.

Erikson, E. H. *Identity: Youth and Crisis.* New York: Norton, 1968.

Fowler, J. W. *Stages of Faith: The Psychology of Human Development and the Quest for Meaning.* New York: HarperCollins, 1981.

Kegan, R. *The Evolving Self: Problem and Process in Human Development.* Cambridge, Mass.: Harvard University Press, 1982.

Kegan, R. *In over Our Heads: The Mental Demands of Modern Life.* Cambridge, Mass.: Harvard University Press, 1994.

King, P. M., and Kitchener, K. S. *Developing Reflective Judgment: Understanding and Promoting Intellectual Growth and Critical Thinking in Adolescents and Adults.* San Francisco: Jossey-Bass, 1994.

Love, P. G., and Guthrie, V. L. *Understanding and Applying Cognitive Development Theory.* New Directions for Student Services, no. 88. San Francisco: Jossey-Bass, 1999.

Parks, S. *The Critical Years: Young Adults and the Search for Meaning, Faith, and Commitment.* New York: HarperCollins, 1986.

Parks, S. *Big Questions, Worthy Dreams: Mentoring Young Adults in Their Search for Meaning, Purpose, and Faith.* San Francisco: Jossey-Bass, 2000.

Perry, W. G., Jr. *Forms of Intellectual and Ethical Development in the College Years: A Scheme.* Orlando: Harcourt Brace, 1970.

Piaget, J. R. *Science of Education and the Psychology of the Child.* New York: Viking, 1969.

PATRICK G. LOVE is associate professor in higher education and student affairs at New York University.

2

*Making career decisions and preparing for life beyond
college are examined from a spiritual perspective.*

Career and Calling: Finding a Place
for the Spirit in Work and Community

Jon C. Dalton

The deepest questions in life are spiritual. They are questions about the
search for ultimate purposes and enduring truths. They are profoundly personal questions that each of us must ultimately answer in our own way:
Why am I here? What am I meant for? What is worth living for? How can
I be for myself and also for others? Whom and what do I serve? What is it
that I love above all else?

Parker Palmer (1998, p. 5) describes spirituality as "an encounter with
otherness." It is a universal instinct toward connection with others and a
discovery of our place in the larger web of life. It is also, as Parker so elo-
quently describes it, a process of turning inward to find where we are at
home with ourselves in an undivided life. The spiritual quest is a lifelong
pursuit, but it emerges full bloom during the transition from youth to adulthood. For most students, the college years are a time of questioning and
spiritual searching in which there is particular emphasis upon two dimensions of spirituality: making connection with ultimate life purpose and finding an inward home. In this chapter, I examine how college students
typically make a spiritual quest in their learning and development in college and how their spirituality influences expectations and preparation for
work and community life beyond college.

NEW DIRECTIONS FOR STUDENT SERVICES, no. 95, Fall 2001   © John Wiley & Sons, Inc.

17

Spirituality and Deeper Learning

It is possible to speak of spirituality as a universal human activity because life is filled with experiences that drive us to question and seek answers on the meaning and purpose of existence. Spirituality is especially important in the learning and experience of college students because late adolescence is a time of heightened sensitivity about personal identity, relationships, ideology, and decisions about the future. It is a time of great potentiality and vulnerability in development, when concerns about individual purpose, meaning, and commitment interact with the forces of cognitive development, maturation, and social expectations. The spiritual domain of the college student's life may well be the most inaccessible facet of personality to outsiders because of its highly inward and personal character. Because of our inclination to treat spiritual matters as a private concern, educators often do not recognize the important role that spirituality has in the learning and development of college students. Students' spiritual reflections and commitments are especially important in helping them to identify and commit to future goals and career choices; this makes spirituality an important consideration when assessing the long-range outcomes of higher education.

To speak of "spirit" or "spirituality" is to enter the realm of inner beliefs and commitments. Most discussion about spirituality in the literature of college student development typically has focused on the religious beliefs and practices of college students and has rarely considered student spirituality as a phenomenon distinct from religion. This distinction can mask the importance of spirituality because many college students interpret religion and spirituality as distinct and separate experiences and identify with them differently. Many students neither participate in organized religious activities nor identify themselves as religious yet attribute great importance to spiritual beliefs and practices. Spirituality is viewed by students as more inclusive and less formal than religion and more personal and individualistic.

Although there has long been interest in the study of religion as an aspect of college student development, only recently has spirituality emerged as an important topic in studying how students learn and grow in college. The spiritual dimension of student learning and development may be considered an aspect of what some now refer to as "deeper learning" because it encompasses not only intellectual knowledge and abilities but also the realm of personal values and convictions. In her recent book, Marcia Mentkowski (Mentkowski and Associates, 2000) describes learning that lasts as an integration of liberal education, education in the professions, and character development. Education that promotes moral character addresses values and moral commitment as learning outcomes of the curriculum and cocurriculum; it seeks to integrate them with intellectual and professional education. Deeper learning is learning that lasts because it touches the deepest feelings and commitments of students and offers a holistic experience of learning that links knowing and feeling.

Spiritual development is a form of deeper learning because it touches on students' encounter with transcendence and ultimate meaning in their lives. Whether it is framed in a religious context, in philosophical questioning, or as a response to experiences of great sadness or joy, most students are compelled to wonder about the purpose of their lives, where their personal journey will take them, and what matters most in the choices they have to make. Education that does not connect with and integrate these spiritual dimensions of learning and development is ultimately less engaging and lasting for a student. Deeper learning, learning that lasts, touches the student's deepest passion and commitment and does so at a time of great openness and possibility for young people. It is this linking of mind and passion at a moment of heightened possibility that makes deeper learning so enduring.

Margaret Mead wrote in her memoirs of her younger years, *Blackberry Winter*, that when she went off to DePauw College in Greencastle, Indiana, she expected a transformation of both mind and spirit: "In college, in some way that I devoutly believed in but could not explain, I expected to become a person" (1972, p. 90). She expected college to somehow clarify and confirm the beliefs and commitments that would define her as a person. She wasn't sure how this all was to happen, but she believed devoutly that college would be the time and place for her to discover who she was and what she should do with the rest of her life. She believed that college held the key to her role and future destiny.

One would not describe Mead's expectations of college as a religious quest because she herself did not affiliate, nor identify, with any formal religion. But her expectations of college surely describe a spiritual quest in which she, like so many young people in college today, saw the college years as the special time and place in which to discover the meaning and purpose of life. Young people are not quite sure just how these revelations will occur, but they devoutly believe that somehow they will.

Spirituality and Personal Destiny

One of the things I like best about college students is their strong sense of personal destiny. Ask most college students about their future and inevitably they talk about a pervasive sense of purpose that is guiding their life into the unknown future. They are uncertain just how their life plan will unfold, but they are convinced that if they search long enough and remain faithful and persistent their life plan will be revealed. This sense of personal destiny, that one is guided by an unfolding life plan or purpose, is a powerful yet often unrecognized aspect of college student learning and development. Erik Erikson (1965), one of the most perceptive observers of youth, wrote that late adolescence is the most idealistic time in life. Youth is the time for dreaming great dreams of a future that is still open, a time when everything seems possible. College students are hesitant to talk about personal topics in casual conversation; they are often made to feel that such talk is out of place in the hard-edged ways of knowing in the academy. But feelings of personal destiny are real for most college students, an important dimension in the process of exploring and confirming career commitments and life plans.

Students' spirituality may be especially important in understanding how they approach career decisions and make long-term commitments about such goals as service to others, family life, and community involvement. In the past, experiencing a deep sense of personal destiny was referred to as a calling. To be called was to have deep inner conviction that one has a personal destiny or future goal that guides life. For students with religious convictions, the belief in calling is often tied to the belief that they are chosen by God for a specific role or task in life. It is a personal calling—a special summons by God to pursue a life role or task.

This religious calling may be perceived either as something quite specific or as an anointing; in the latter case one's life is blessed for some special but unknown future purpose. My observation is that most college students have a strong sense of personal destiny or calling that is deeply personal and often unspoken. Perhaps this sense is the inevitable by-product of high expectations, youthful uncertainty, and the search for identity in late adolescence.

In *The Spiritual Quest: Transcendence in Myth, Religion, and Science* (1994), Robert Torrance argues that young adults especially are inclined to a spiritual quest because they recognize the limitations, uncertainty, and potentiality of their situation. Although college students tend to struggle at some time with deciding on majors and future careers, most have an inner sense that they are meant to do something special with their lives, if they can just discover the personal path that leads through the apparent maze of alternatives and possibilities.

It is important to recognize faith in personal destiny in college students because it is often a deeply sustaining conviction that supports them through one of the greatest periods of uncertainty in their lives. Moreover, it should remind us that helping college students make choices about majors and careers involves much more than matching aptitudes and interests with job options. It also involves exploration with students of their sense of personal calling and destiny to understand their deepest values and commitments for their future.

The Neglect of Spirituality in Higher Education

What are colleges and universities doing today to encourage students' spiritual development? Are these schools committed to helping students clarify and confirm beliefs and commitments that define them profoundly? Are they committed to helping students discover who they are and what they should do with the rest of their lives? Certainly, most faith-based colleges and universities have been engaged in encouraging spiritual growth as an important part of their institutional mission for a long time. But what about the secular ones? Some of our most thoughtful educational leaders have been calling attention to the failure of American higher education to address these educational and spiritual questions. Ernest Boyer (1995) wrote in his progress report on American colleges that "the nation's colleges have been less attentive to the larger, more transcendent issues that give meaning to existence and help students put their own lives in perspective" (p. 29).

In recent years, one of the strongest statements about the importance of moral and civic learning came in a Kellogg Foundation report (1997), "Returning to Our Roots: The Student Experience." The report argues that "the biggest educational challenge we face revolves around developing character, conscience, citizenship, tolerance, civility, and individual and social responsibility in our students. We dare not ignore this obligation in a society that sometimes gives the impression that virtues such as these are discretionary. These should be a part of the standard equipment of our graduates, not options" (p. 13).

Frank Newman, director of the Futures Project funded by the Pew Charitable Trusts, writes that the "most enduring role for the university has been the socialization of young people for their roles in society" (2000, p. 11). He expresses grave concern about the heavy emphasis on workforce skills and for-profit activities in colleges and universities.

Despite their much-publicized desire for money and status, college students also express great interest in helping others, finding a guiding philosophy of life, and contributing to their community. Students have high expectations for both economic and personal success, and for making a difference in the lives of others. They exhibit cynicism about politics and civic leadership. There remains good reason to worry that college students are opting for lives of privatism and consumption at the expense of ethical and spiritual values.

Again my own observation of college students is somewhat different. I do not believe that most of them regard personal ambition and moral commitment as mutually exclusive, or even in direct conflict with one another. Perhaps it is the idealism and energy of youth that makes it possible for students to believe that they can have it all and do it all. They can achieve the good life of wealth and status while living a good life of moral commitment and service to others. These two types of ambition and lifestyle are not seen by college students to be mutually exclusive. Indeed, many students believe that wealth and status are the necessary means for making an important contribution to social welfare and justice. Moreover, college students often demonstrate their commitment to both while in college by balancing their studies and personal pursuits with community service activities and other forms of religious and moral commitment.

I find students eager to talk about their lives and what matters most to them: their families, their doubts and uncertainties, their hopes and fears with respect to the future, and their desire to make a difference and be true to their deepest beliefs and convictions. They are eager to talk about values and beliefs and to explore their public and private responsibilities. Yet many students find that in higher education such ethical and spiritual concerns are often relegated to the personal realm; they feel awkward or embarrassed to talk about them publicly. Rather than helping students link head and heart, intellectual and ethical development, we often force an isolation of these two important domains of students' learning and development in higher education. When the domains of learning and development are separated, the atmosphere for students can appear indifferent, and even callused, as if what they believe in and care about is somehow irrelevant to the life of the mind.

How to Encourage Spiritual Growth

One of the best ways in which college students nurture the link between head and heart in college is through community service. Daloz, Keen, Keen, and Parks (1996) report in their research on individuals who have a high level of commitment to serving others that the call to service is a spiritual imperative. Service helps young people experience a sense of purpose in a changing and diverse world. Through the experience of caring for others and taking responsibility for helping to solve social problems, students are better able to stay in touch with their moral feelings and beliefs. Caring for others helps them recognize and experience the connection between intellectual and moral beliefs and the reality of acting on those values in a real-life moral situation.

Students report that participating in service activity helps to broaden their understanding of people and their circumstances; it causes them to be more introspective about their own beliefs and values. Despite the fact that students often encounter serious and intractable problems in their service role, these experiences do not seem to diminish their idealism or moral conviction. The connection with real people caught in difficult life circumstances who need support helps to humanize the student's moral beliefs and to foster a sense of practical virtue.

For many students, the experience of seeing social problems in a deeply human context, up close and personal, is life changing. Beliefs are forged into commitments that have long-range implications for career and lifestyle decisions. Learning is experienced in a new context and with a new purpose. Anyone who has witnessed the impact of a powerful moral experience in the life of a college student knows how transforming it can be.

The threat of such heavy and sustained emphasis on material and self-interested values in college can lead to gradual erosion of moral and spiritual commitment. Given the escalating stress of achieving career goals and the relentless hedonism of popular culture, it is not surprising that the values of college students have become increasingly privatistic and self-centered during the 1990s. Colleges, for their part, have exacerbated this situation through heavy marketing of the economic and career advantages of higher education as their most important outcomes. These messages are not lost on students, who are perceptive enough to recognize the persistent themes of wealth and status in the academic as well as popular culture.

When Spirituality Becomes Self-Centered

In the *Chronicle of Higher Education,* Donna Schafer (2000) argues that religion on campus has become a form of counseling in which religion and God are ignored. Spirituality, she states, promotes an internal feel-goodism that only infrequently inspires dedication to some higher claim.

The argument that spirituality is a kind of inner-directed feel-good movement that makes no moral claim on students, nor links them to some sense of the sacred, is an important warning against using spirituality as a kind of ubiquitous self-serving therapy for students. A spiritual quest that focuses primarily on self-definition and self-understanding fails to consider equally serious concerns about relationships with others and the search for transcendence that are central to that quest. If spirituality is regarded as essentially a private and introspective process, a kind of private journey of the soul, in which few if any moral claims are made upon the spiritual traveler, then the claim of spirituality as feel-goodism has some validity. Self-understanding and acceptance are important outcomes of spirituality, but I think we fail as educators if we do not help students link the ethical claims of life and work with others to one's relationship with what is transcendent and sacred.

I have seen in a lifetime of working with college students that it is not a concern for feel-goodism that drives them to reflect on spiritual questions, but rather the relentless and fundamental questions they encounter about purpose and direction in their lives. College students typically find themselves at a crucial point in life, having to make major decisions about life choice and direction yet having few structured opportunities in higher education to examine the spiritual implications of such big decisions. If we do our job well in higher education, then students inevitably reflect upon the greater purpose of their lives. They ask questions about worthy commitment, moral responsibility, and life's inevitable transcendent claims and experiences. I am less concerned about the potential feel-goodism of spirituality efforts since the questions and impulses that lead students to pursue spiritual awareness and development naturally push them to ethical and religious issues.

College students who are able to continue their spiritual development in college and to integrate their deepest beliefs and passions with career and life plans are able to make the transition from college to work and life in community satisfyingly and successfully. They are able to measure the worth of their work and contributions not only in terms of financial and material benefits but also from the perspective of personal fulfillment and satisfaction on the basis of personal spiritual beliefs and conviction. There is persuasive evidence that individuals who live principled lives, lives of character and spirituality, are able to succeed in work settings and social relationships because the qualities of integrity, commitment, and respect for others are so valued in today's society (Covey, 1995).

Many, if not most, of the self-improvement and personal success publications that are so popular today and used so heavily in business are based upon a model of life and leadership in which core ethical principles and an undivided inner and outer life are the most important features. A term that is increasingly used for this form of moral and values-centered lifestyle is "character." Character is a concept that has been around for a long time, at least since the ancient Greeks and the writing of Aristotle. But it is being used with new emphasis to define a type of belief system and lifestyle that is based upon moral principles in which an individual achieves great consistency between belief and behavior. Spirituality is an important feature of character since spiritual practice is one of the important ways that one enriches the inner life, transcends self-centeredness, and moves toward an undivided life.

One outcome of a higher education that integrates spirituality with intellectual and personal development is a committed life of moral and civic responsibility. College students who are able to develop their moral convictions and integrate their beliefs into career choices and lifestyle patterns are likely to be active participants in social and civic communities. Such civic activism is essential in our political and social system since democracy requires citizen participation and commitment to such core values as justice, fairness, respect for others, and the common good. Higher education that ignores the spiritual dimension of learning and development not only inhibits students' quest for the good life but it makes it less likely that graduates will be engaged citizens willing to do the long and arduous work of creating a good society.

References

Boyer, E. "Making a Commitment to Character." *Principal,* Sept. 1995, pp. 28–31.

Covey, S. *The Seven Habits of Highly Effective People.* New York: Simon and Schuster, 1995.

Daloz, L. A., Keen, C. H., Keen, J. P., and Parks, S. D. *Common Fire.* Boston: Beacon Press, 1996.

Erikson, E. *The Challenge of Youth.* New York: Doubleday, 1965.

Kellogg Foundation Report. *Returning to Our Roots: The Student Experience.* Battle Creek, Mich.: Kellogg Foundation, 1997.

Mead, M. *Blackberry Winter: My Earliest Years.* New York: Morrow, 1972.

Mentkowski, M., and Associates. *Learning That Lasts.* San Francisco: Jossey-Bass, 2000.

Newman, F. "Saving Higher Education's Soul." *Change,* 2000, *33*(5), pp. 16–23.

Palmer, P. J. *The Courage to Teach*. San Francisco: Jossey-Bass, 1998.

Schafer, D. "Me-First Spirituality Is a Sorry Substitute for Organized Religion on Campuses." *Chronicle of Higher Education*, Aug. 2000, A12.

Torrance, R. M. *The Spiritual Quest: Transcendence in Myth, Religion, and Science*. Berkeley: University of California Press, 1994.

JON C. DALTON *is the former vice president for student affairs at Florida State University and is on the faculty there in the Educational Leadership Program.*

3

This chapter connects the concept of soul to organizational theory and models for student affairs work.

Infusing Soul into Student Affairs: Organizational Theory and Models

Kathleen Manning

It is difficult to speculate about the sudden rise of religion and spirituality on college campuses. Perhaps the interest is the result of aging baby boomers becoming more introspectively reflective. Perhaps members of generation X are abandoning materialism and thinking metaphysically. More speculatively, perhaps the postmodern world has left us weary for some meaning-making activity that takes us outside our relative, self-centered thoughts and concerns. Regardless of the reasons, spirituality has gained a foothold on college campuses.

The interest in spirituality is reflected in books recently published or repopularized. Among these are *SQ: Connecting with Our Spiritual Intelligence* by Danah Zohar and Ian Marshall (2000), the *Chicken Soup for the Soul* series, Rachael Kessler's *The Soul of Education* (2000), and Gary Zukav's *The Seat of the Soul* (1989). One could argue that the Harry Potter series, with its otherworldly occurrences, follows the interest of students, staff, and faculty in spirit and magic.

Perhaps stranger than even Harry's magical feats is the emergence of the topic of soul and spirit in educational organizational theory. Lee Bolman and Terrence Deal (*Leading with Soul*, 1995), well-known authors in the area of educational administration, write about a man's spiritual journey after realizing that his work life no longer had meaning. The book, a fable about the danger of losing your self in your work, stands in stark contrast to their textbooks about the procedural aspects of organizational theory (Bolman and Deal, 1984, 1997).

More off the beaten path, Alan Briskin's thought-provoking work, *The Stirring of Soul in the Workplace* (1996), put words to the growing desire to incorporate soul into public institutional life, including that of corporations. These spiritual trends are a natural fit in student affairs administration, where meaning making, introspection, distinctiveness, and character have long held significance.

This chapter discusses the topic of spirituality in organizational theory and student affairs practice. I review theories and models presented in Bolman and Deal (1995) and Briskin (1996) and apply them to student affairs administration. The word *soul* is defined and discussed as a means to provide context for this discussion.

Soul: The Underworld and the Upperworld

Soul is often associated and confused with such words as spirit, sacredness, and spirituality. These terms point to a religious approach to soul, but in this chapter I adopt a secular, anthropological connotation. The emphasis instead is on how human beings create meaning in their lives using an idea of "soul [that] speaks in the language of metaphor, fantasy, and emotion" (Briskin, 1996, p. 10). Soul, "the indefinable essence of a person's spirit and being" (Whyte, 1994, p. 13), involves a journey of the self that "is indirect, circular, metaphorical, imbued with a richness and confusion evoking our deepest longings and most profound fears" (Briskin, 1996, p. xx).

Briskin traced definitions of soul across history. The ancient Greek perspective viewed it as an aspect of the underworld, "a place of depth and shadowy realities" (1996, p. 11). The soul as a reflection of the underworld connects humans with the unconscious aspects of human living. The Hebrews offered a second perspective, believing it was associated with vitality, animation, essence, and renewal. The Taoists, similar to the Hebrews, considered the soul to be a place where a union of opposites could occur. Spirit and matter, light and dark, and good and evil could be expressed, conflicted, and perhaps reconciled in the soul. Bolman and Deal (1995) hold a fourth perspective on soul, saying it contains a spark of the divine. Each philosophical tradition regards soul as including positive and negative aspects of human living. These two sides of the human soul can be defined as the underworld and the upperworld.

The Soul's Upper- and Underworlds

The soul's upperworld speaks to the emotionally optimistic and psychologically affirmative ideals of beauty, joy, connection, happiness, and pleasure. Among others, professionals in student affairs often associate these concepts with healthy human living. In fact, we overuse the concept of healthfulness to such a point that any sadness, depression (temporary or otherwise), and unhappiness are seen as unhealthy and in need of "curing." Only the "upper-world" of the soul is to be shared in public, organizational life. Student affairs educators in particular are to be cheerful and accommodating at all times. The goal is to express "ease, delight, and celebration" (O'Donohue, 1997, p. 125).

Modern business life arises from a love of the upperworld, of material products, of order and organization; it celebrates the material, light-filled portion of existence. It is the world as we see it (or as we would like to see it) and as it most makes sense to us. But as many of us suspect in sensing the shock waves now traveling through our corporations and institutions, it is only half the story (Whyte, 1994).

The "underworld," in contrast, is the place from which people experience feelings of abandonment, rage, guilt, despair, and shame. Many of us actively avoid, deny, and go to great lengths to avoid these underworld feelings. Any expression, particularly public, of these very real human feelings is viewed as weakness. Underworld emotions, though normal and complementary to expression of the positive upperworld feelings, are discouraged or even banished from modern organizations.

But the underworld of the soul can be viewed positively: "To become aware of the shadow is to seek not only self-knowledge but also a portal to the larger world in which we live" (Briskin, 1996, p. 45). It is within the borders of the underworld that the "primal energy of our soul holds a wonderful warmth and welcome for us" (O'Donohue, 1997, p. 100). Student affairs educators, too, are only truly whole when they make meaning in their lives by embracing both the upperworld and the underworld of human living. Without the normal—though painful—human emotions of the underworld, the positive upperworld of the soul cannot be appreciated or expressed. One must have known sadness to possess happiness, live through grief to understand joy, and recognize pain to value delight. Human beings, in their public and private lives, can fully express the underworld and upperworld of the soul to fully know human living.

Soul and Organizational Living

It may seem incongruous to connect soul with organizational theories and models, particularly bureaucracy. Historically, an organization has been a professional, objective place devoid of emotion, feeling, and personal concerns. Frederick Taylor (1911), the father of the efficiency-obsessed models of scientific management viewed feelings—in fact, any sign of being human—as superfluous in corporate practice. According to the mechanistic approach to bureaucracy (Morgan, 1986), organizational life is often routinized with the precision demanded of clockwork. People are frequently expected to arrive at work at a given time, perform a predetermined set of activities, rest at appointed hours, and then resume their tasks until work is over. In many organizations, one shift of workers replaces another in methodical fashion so that work can continue uninterrupted twenty-four hours a day, every day of the year. Often the work is wholly mechanical and repetitive. The employee is in essence expected to behave as if part of a machine (Morgan, 1986).

As such, people cannot and should not express their whole being (that is, mind, body, spirit) at work. Rather, they should abandon their whole selves, particularly their spiritual side, as they perform their work in an organization; any organization "has criteria for membership. Those who don't meet the criteria are excluded, but just as important, those who are included exclude much of themselves from the organization" (Zohar and Marshall, 2000, p. 103).

Exchanging Soul for Salary

Through abandoning their whole selves, people exchange labor for a salary. To complete this exchange, they must sacrifice their human tendency to generously give time, dedicate effort, and engage in creative action. Instead, they work toward organizational goals (for example, profit, progress, growth) through means (such as competition) that may be at best barely associated with joy, accomplishment, or a positive sense of self. Our modern organizations, especially those fashioned after the machine model of Frederick Taylor, have asked us to sacrifice too much in their service. Theorists such as Briskin purport that "people cannot simply become mechanisms of production without losing connection with their own experience: fragility, wonder, passion, and mystery. These qualities are critical to health, creativity, and compassion for others" (1996, p. 134).

Although most people long for happiness over pain, joy over depression, and cooperation over conflict, a problem emerges when underworld feelings are denied within an organization. "If we design organizations only with the upperworld in mind, we are less able to account for the tremors that are set off from below" (Briskin, 1996, p. xvii). Without recognition that there is pain, despair, and depression, these "tremors" will emerge in potentially dangerous ways: absenteeism, irritability, and burnout. With emphasis on the mirror images of the upperworld and underworld of the soul, members of an organization can identify areas in which balance, wholeness, and authenticity are obvious. The question for us student affairs educators, as we approach our work in a more integrated and holistic fashion, is how to express all parts of our humanity—and soul—in the service of our communities.

The Soul of Student Affairs Practice

Anyone who has worked in student affairs understands the potential in the field for great joy. In preparing a speech to be delivered to student activities professionals, I asked some of them to tell me why they continued to work in the field. Among their many reasons, respondents cited the opportunity to make a difference, the capacity to work for social justice, the power to transform others' lives and their own, the challenge inherent in the work, and the community of close colleagues with whom they worked (Manning, 2000b). Such reasons, combined with the foundational purpose of the field, give student affairs educators the opportunity to infuse soul into their practice. Here is a list of everyday expressions in the field that have to do with the upperworld of the soul:

The opportunity to experience great joy from student affairs work
The sense of accomplishment possible when involved with educating students
The possibility of career satisfaction that is not solely linked to materialism
The chance to celebrate students' success and our own
The pursuit of a lifestyle marked by health and wellness

These soulful and spiritual aspects of the profession express the essence of student affairs practice. Although they represent compelling reasons to enter and persist in the student affairs field, as Briskin (1996) discussed there is also an underworld or shadow side to the organization. Without attention to the underside of student affairs administration, the negative elements of this aspect of human living leak out, and one is unable to attend to its effects positively. This list suggests the hidden elements of the underworld of the soul in student affairs:

Impatience with students and staff
Workaholism and exhaustion
Territoriality (us versus them), a competitive view of the institution
The danger of entering into codependent relationships
Lack of balanced work and play lives

As with any human service profession, student affairs administrators are inclined to enter into codependent relationships. In these interactions, a person can lose track of his or her needs in the service of another. It is difficult to set limits when a codependent educator sees himself or herself as the only person who can solve the problem, provide the answer, or complete the task. With an overinflated view of one's importance in the organization, any administrator can fall into the "ease" of unilateral decisions without participation or counsel from community members.

Good and bad, student affairs educators must attend to both aspects of the soul. If only the positive side of the soul is expressed, we risk losing meaning, beauty, fragility, union, wildness, and divinity (Briskin, 1996). Embracing contradictions allows us to see a greater range of human living: hierarchy and cooperation, workaholism and a healthy lifestyle, elitism and equity, bureaucracy and chaos, and personal and professional. The goal is to listen to the wisdom of the shadow side of the soul. Through this deep listening, student affairs educators are exposed to the soul's creative polarity. As such, they can be this *and* that, compassionate *and* cruel, negative *and* positive, soft *and* hard.

Spiritual Journeys Within Student Affairs

Humans are meaning-making beings. Whether one adheres to Socrates' admonition to "know thyself" or advice that the "unexamined life is not worth living," humans possess a hunger to create meaning within their lives. Youth and inexperience might betray their motives, but students also possess a hunger to create meaning in their lives. The close proximity of student affairs administrators and students opens countless opportunities for administrators to encourage expression of meaning within students' lives.

One of the means through which to express soul in the student affairs workplace is to attend to the everyday spiritual journey that is part of human living. Table 3.1 outlines some examples of the spiritual journey and how it is expressed on campus.

Student affairs educators often become involved in this variety of educational practice thanks to their own personal transformation as students. Someone affected them deeply, and they now strongly desire to be involved in another's life to the same degree. Discussion concerning soul can remind the student affairs educator that the spiritual journey of transformation, spirit, and intellectual wonder is an everyday occurrence. As educators, we can be reflective so that the spiritual journey is not overlooked amid our zeal for administrative efficiency or disciplinary control.

Remaining aware of the spiritual journey and expression of soul on the college campus is made more difficult by the fragmentation and specialization encouraged within academia. Academic departments, majors, and faculty research specialties are prime examples of this specialization. Student affairs administrators are mimicking the academic system as they divide their functional areas into smaller and smaller units. The spiritual journey is also in danger of falling prey to the human desire (also prevalent within student affairs) to examine only the upperworld of the soul.

Leadership Models

Similarly to Briskin, Bolman and Deal (1995) are organizational theorists whose work reached beyond the technical aspects of institutional life. Their book *Leading with Soul* is a fable. Steve is disillusioned with a work life that previously gave him significant meaning; he is looking to find his way again. He consults a wise sage, Maria, who helps him reconnect with the spiritual side of human living. The authors offer several conclusions about soul, leadership, and organizations, notably that (1) traditional "hero/heroine" style leadership has left educators, administrative staff, and organizations tired and disempowered; and (2) true leadership requires that you "lead from something deep in your heart" (Bolman and Deal, 1995, p. 21).

Bolman and Deal discuss leadership in terms of gifts, not as a set of skills, personal qualities, or circumstances. Rather, "leadership is giving.

Table 3.1. The Spiritual Journey in Student Affairs

Source of Spirit	Example in Student Affairs Practice
Meaning and purpose	Student affairs a "calling," not a job
Reverence and wonder	Pursuit of intellectual quest
Common humanity	Service learning, community development
Sacredness of life	Respect for diverse others, social justice action
Mission and calling	Dedication to student learning

Leadership is an ethic, a gift of oneself" (1995, p. 102). Four specific gifts of love, power, authorship, and significance are emphasized.

The first gift, of love, means that the leader finds out what matters to others. This gift focuses on sharing, knowing the people with whom the leader works, and caring deeply about their lives. The second gift, power, means that the leader does not bestow power from a position of authority but builds an organization where all can be empowered. Leaders who offer the gift of power share their responsibilities with others so that all have the opportunity to grow, achieve, and flourish. The third gift, authorship, means the leader does not supervise another's work in an authoritarian way but builds autonomy so others see their work as meaningful and worthwhile. The gift of significance means that the leader fully understands that people possess the capacity to create their work together. Celebration of these achievements is an aspect of this last gift. College campuses are rich with ceremonies, rituals, symbols, and traditions that represent spirit, engender celebration, and urge meaning making (Manning, 1994, 2000a).

The four gifts of love, power, authorship, and significance are congruent with our profession's founding values of whole-person development, understanding of differences, and achieving all that the student is able. The journey of the soul that is central to meaning making within student affairs includes identity development, social justice, student leadership, service learning, and friendships.

Suggestions for Infusing Soul into an Organization

Student affairs educators can use a set of questions, authored by David Trott (2000), to think about how to infuse soul and spirituality into their work with students, staff, administrators, and faculty:

How is your spirit enthused by work?
What occurs during the course of an ordinary workday that bolsters our sense of spirituality?
If you had the freedom to create a spiritually healthy organization of your choosing, what would you emphasize?

Do you feel as though work serves any higher or greater purpose than
  accomplishing the tasks at hand?
Describe an inspirational person in your present work setting.
What do you do when you feel the need for a spiritual boost while at work?

With these questions as a guide, and using the next set of suggestions
for practice as a catalyst, student affairs educators can infuse soul into their
educational organizations and leadership practice.

• *Strive for balance.* This is not meant as a suggestion to balance time,
task, and responsibilities. Infusing soul into our work is an attempt to achieve
balance by crafting both a life and a career. When professionals lose their balance between work and play, they also lose their capacity to express the soul.
Students need to learn this balance, and we can serve as role models for them.

• *Emphasize* both/and *rather than* either-or. Western culture has taught
us to view the world dualistically. People educated in Western ways see life
as black or white, right or wrong, up or down, work or play. New science
organizational theorists (Wheatley, 1994; Whyte, 1994; Zohar and Marshall,
2000) urge us to view the world as much more complex. This complexity
includes images of the soul within the organization, images that are too
complex for the simplistic logic of dualism.

• *Embrace wholeness—even the negative, painful aspects.* To express the
soul within an organization, educators and administrators can seek unity
and integration within themselves and their institution: "The soul adores
unity. What you separate, the soul joins" (O'Donohue, 1997, p. 118). An
aspect of this embrace is to befriend the negative (O'Donohue, 1997). To
embrace wholeness, one has to face the negative or underworld of the soul.

• *Make room for silence.* Modern life is characterized by an amazing
cacophony of voices, sounds, noises, and distractions; as O'Donohue writes
further, "one of the reasons so many people are suffering from stress is not
that they are doing stressful things but that they allow so little time for
silence" (1997, p. 109). Bringing soul into the organization may mean that
we have to make room for silence as well.

• *Create a language to express the meaning that is at home in the soul.* Some
sources for thinking about soul (religious traditions, new age spirituality) ring
false for administrators: "Many of the words we use are of the fast-food spiritual variety. These words are too thick to echo experience; they are too weak
to bring the inner mystery of things to real expression" (O'Donohue, 1997,
pp. 66–67). Rather than using what exists, perhaps we have to create a new
language to express how one remains whole within an organization.

• *Embrace playfulness.* In a classic book about higher education organizational theory, Cohen and March (1974) encourage leaders to be more
playful. "Playfulness is a deliberate, temporary relaxation of the rules," they
say, "in order to explore the possibilities of alternative rules. When we are
playful, we challenge the necessity of consistency" (p. 225).

Summary

Student affairs educators are urged to embrace the whole-person view of themselves joyfully, a view we have traditionally believed was important for students (American Council on Education, 1937). Such a view may help us instill soul into our work and organizations, toward the goal of creating more unity, decreasing the level of burnout, encouraging balance, and educating students completely.

References

American Council on Education. *The Student Personnel Point of View.* (American Council on Education Studies, series 1, no. 3.) Washington, D.C.: American Council on Education, 1937.

Bolman, L. G., and Deal, T. L. *Modern Approaches to Understanding and Managing Organizations.* San Francisco: Jossey-Bass, 1984.

Bolman, L. G., and Deal, T. L. *Leading with Soul: An Uncommon Journey of Spirit.* San Francisco: Jossey-Bass, 1995.

Bolman, L. G., and Deal, T. L. *Reframing Organizations: Artistry, Choice, and Leadership.* (2nd ed.) San Francisco: Jossey-Bass, 1997.

Briskin, A. *The Stirring of Soul in the Workplace.* San Francisco: Jossey-Bass, 1996.

Cohen, M. D., and March, J. G. *Leadership and Ambiguity: The American College President.* New York: McGraw-Hill, 1974.

Kessler, R. *The Soul of Education: Helping Students Find Connection, Compassion, and Character at School.* Alexandria, Va.: Association for Supervision and Curriculum Development, 2000.

Manning, K. "Rituals and Rescission: Building Community in Hard Times." *Journal of College Student Development,* 1994, *35*(4), 275–281.

Manning, K. *Rituals, Ceremonies, and Cultural Meaning in Higher Education.* (Critical Issues Series, Henry Giroux, series eds.) Westport, Conn.: Greenwood Press, 2000a.

Manning, K. "Why I'm (Still) Here: The Ups and Down of a Career in Student Affairs." Speech presented at the National Association for Campus Activities, Marlborough, Mass., Nov. 2000b.

Morgan, G. *Images of Organization.* Thousand Oaks, Calif.: Sage, 1986.

O'Donohue, J. *Anam Cara: A Book of Celtic Wisdom.* New York: HarperCollins, 1997.

Taylor, F. *Principles of Scientific Management.* New York: HarperCollins, 1911.

Trott, D. Comments presented at Going Public with Spirituality in Higher Education, University of Massachusetts, Amherst, June 2000.

Wheatley, M. *Leadership and the New Science: Learning About Organization from an Orderly Universe.* San Francisco: Berrett-Koehler, 1994.

Whyte, D. *The Heart Aroused.* New York: Currency Doubleday, 1994.

Zohar, D., and Marshall, I. *SQ: Connecting with Our Spiritual Intelligence.* New York: Bloomsbury, 2000.

Zukav, G. *The Seat of the Soul.* New York: Simon and Schuster, 1989.

KATHLEEN MANNING is associate professor in higher education and student affairs at the University of Vermont.

4

It is important for student affairs practitioners to explore consideration of legal restraints on religious expression on the college campus. Relevant cases are discussed and examples are given.

The Law and Spirituality: How the Law Supports and Limits Expression of Spirituality on the College Campus

R. Thomas Clark

The mission statements of many colleges and universities speak of developing the whole person of the student, including the mind, body, and spirit. Clearly, the academic efforts of an institution address development of the mind. Just as clearly, the athletic and recreation programs located in the academic activities, in a department of athletics, or in student life seek to develop the body of the student. However, other than campus ministry, it is often difficult to identify the departments or programs that are devoted to developing the spirit. The culture of the campus, whether it be a strictly secular institution or one that is affiliated with an organized religion, is frequently significant in developing the spirit of the student. Recently published research by Astin and Antonio (2000) indicates that sectarian institutions generally have a positive effect on developing character in their students.

This chapter identifies the legal principles and constraints that apply to expression of spirituality on the college campus by members of the community, be they students or employees. The chapter is not intended to offer legal advice. The law of a particular state, county, and city may affect the discussion significantly. The reader is encouraged to consult with competent local counsel to ascertain the relevant law of the jurisdiction and its application on a particular campus. This chapter is not intended to be a legal treatise or an exhaustive discussion of the legal issues pertaining to spirituality and religion on college campuses.

Instead, my intention is to address the hesitancy heard from student affairs professionals who are unaware of or confused about the legal issues involved in religion and spirituality on the college campus. This includes their role as student life professionals in various programs and services, and their own desire to explore spirituality in the workplace. This has been experienced, for instance, in the criticism of using campuswide e-mail to announce a luncheon discussion group about faith issues. Attendees at regional and national conferences have noted a lack of connection between spirituality and student development, as seen in the wellness models we use for programming. There appears to be general confusion about expression of faith-based beliefs on college campuses. I hope this chapter gives the reader guidance to engage in a campus dialogue where the law both limits and encourages expression of spiritual or faith beliefs.

In using the term *spirituality,* I clearly intend that the reader understand it differently from *religion. Spirituality* refers to that noncorporal aspect of each human being that is separate from the mind. *Religion* refers to an organized set of doctrines around faith beliefs within an organization. There may be some congruence between spirituality and religion, but there are also some distinctions. Spiritual development may occur without an individual being a member of any organized religion. Development of one's spirit may be aided (or in some cases impeded) by membership in a religious organization. My purpose here is not to advance any particular set of religious beliefs but to discuss the legal implications regarding expression of the spirituality on campus.

Overview of Legal Principles

It may be helpful to further distinguish between the definitions of *religion* and *spirituality* from a legal perspective. The U.S. Supreme Court and other courts following its lead have for years struggled consistently with what constitutes a religion. The reason for the struggle is both historical and cultural in nature. It is well known that those seeking religious freedom established many of the original colonies. Puritans settled in Massachusetts as well as New Hampshire and Connecticut. Catholics settled in Maryland. Quakers settled in Pennsylvania. In establishing a government that guaranteed freedom of religion, the framers of the U.S. Constitution struggled in meeting what seemingly are competing goals: how to guarantee freedom of expression of religious beliefs without placing the government in the position of declaring what are acceptable religions or placing one religion above all others.

This task is made more complicated by the nature of American society, one in which religion seems to be imbedded in our culture. One only needs to examine our currency, our Pledge of Allegiance, and our legal holidays (for example, Christmas) to see the spiritual influence on our culture. Indeed, the Supreme Court has articulated as much in deciding cases involving display of holiday symbols on government property by a rule of law that has been dubbed "the reindeer rule." That is, are Santa Claus and his reindeer in a different category from a crèche or menorah? Are they religious, or are they a reflection of our culture?

Constitutionally, there are two provisions of the First Amendment that apply to the issues of religion and spirituality: the establishment clause and the free-expression clause. The establishment clause was intended to prevent a state of affairs as existed in England, where Henry VIII decreed that the Church of England was the official state religion in which all citizens must be members. The establishment clause states that "Congress shall make no law respecting an establishment of religion." Over the years, the term *Congress* has been interpreted by the U.S. Supreme Court to mean all bodies of a government, be they federal, state, or local, and be they legislative, executive, or judicial in function.

The second provision of the First Amendment that applies to religion and spirituality, the free-exercise clause, was intended to prevent the government (again, federal, state, or local, including legislative, executive, or judicial function) from interfering with a citizen's expression of religious or spiritual beliefs. This clause, immediately following the establishment clause, reads "Congress shall make no law . . . prohibiting the free exercise thereof (religion)." In seeking to meet at the same time the task of guaranteeing free expression of religious beliefs while not establishing a religion, the Supreme Court has established essentially a two-part test: Are the beliefs sincerely held by a follower? Do the beliefs occupy the same central space in the believer's life as traditional religious beliefs occupy in the traditional believer's life? If both parts of this test are satisfied, then the law accords the beliefs protection intended by the First Amendment.

The first question clearly is a difficult one for anyone to decide. How sincerely beliefs are held may be a subjective determination, but indicators include the length of time the beliefs have been held by the individual, or the characteristics of the beliefs. For instance, do the beliefs include a day of worship, a place of worship, a holy book, a set of dogma, a leader of the group, a belief in an afterlife, and so on? Were the beliefs learned as a child, or accepted later in life?

Application

These principles apply to colleges and universities differently, depending upon whether the institution is operated by the state or is a private institution. The limitations contained in the amendments to the Constitution apply to governmental action and not to that of private institutions or individuals. Therefore, public institutions are subject to much scrutiny regarding issues of expression of religion and spirituality. However, limitations do apply to privately operated institutions. Congress has passed a number of statutes with similar provisions to those contained in the Constitution that apply to private organizations. One such prominent statute is the Civil Rights Act of

1964 as amended. It prohibits discrimination in employment on the basis of race, color, creed, national origin, gender, marital status, pregnancy, and wealth. As such, behavior that would be prohibited by the First Amendment as applied to publicly operated colleges may also be prohibited for a private college as applied to its employees under the Civil Rights Act. This act does not apply to students, however.

The provisions of the Civil Rights Act as well as the First Amendment are not absolute. In fact, each states that the religious beliefs must be "reasonably accommodated." What constitutes a reasonable accommodation is a matter of fact given the specific circumstances of each situation. For instance, what if a faculty member's religious beliefs prohibit work on the Sabbath, a day in which classes are conducted? Must the faculty member teach a class? May an institution discipline or terminate a faculty member who refuses to work on this day? Are there "accommodations" to the faculty member's religious beliefs that can reasonably be made?

Prominent in resolving questions of whether the law supports or limits the expression of spirituality on sectarian college campuses is application of the three-prong test of *Lemon* v. *Kurtzman* (1971). The Supreme Court enunciated this test: "First, the statute must have a secular legislative purpose; second, its principal or primary effect must be one that neither advances nor inhibits religion; . . . finally the statute must not foster an excessive government entanglement with religion." For instance, in *Smith* v. *Board of Governors of North Carolina* (1977), the U.S. district court was presented with the question of whether a program of state funds for tuition grants and scholarships for students attending private church-related institutions violates the establishment clause of the First Amendment. Under the program, no funds were allowed for any student pursuing a course of study primarily designed to prepare that student for a career in a religious vocation. In this case, after applying the *Lemon* test the Court concluded that there was no violation of the First Amendment.

Illustrative Cases

In addressing the areas where the law, either under constitutional principles or statutory provisions, supports expression of spirituality, I offer several as examples to guide application of these principles.

Student-Led Spontaneous Prayer: Prayer at School Ceremonies. The principles governing whether students may engage in prayer on school property can be examined by a number of illustrative cases. In 1999, a student uttered a brief prayer immediately prior to making a class presentation. The student was instructed by the professor to stop the prayer and not to pray in class again. The president of the community college involved indicated that the incident reflected general confusion over what constituted appropriate religious expression in the classroom (McMurtrie, 2000).

It has been common practice for schools at all levels to include an invocation or benediction as a part of a graduation ceremony. Whether an invocation is consistent with legal requirements depends on whether the institution is a college or an elementary or high school. Indiana University was challenged to eliminate the invocation and benediction as part of its commencement exercise. In this case, the U.S. district court held that a public university might include an invocation and a benediction at such a ceremony. The court noted that "given the nonsectarian and brief nature of the invocation and benediction, as well as the sophistication of the audience and university setting, we find that adherents and nonadherents alike could not perceive the two prayers as either endorsing or denigrating their particular religious choices or religion generally." However, the result may be substantially different for an elementary or high school graduation ceremony.

In recent years, the Supreme Court has heard cases that dealt with the issue of prayers at high school graduation and other events. In its first major case on the issue, the Court held that clergy are not permitted under the First Amendment to give an invocation or benediction at a high school graduation ceremony (*Lee* v. *Weisman,* 112 S. Ct., 1992). However, in *Lee* the Court indicated that student-led prayers at graduation are permissible, as they are not an action of the school, in and of itself. However, the Court most recently has clarified—and created confusion—with another ruling in this regard. The Court held that school-sponsored, student-led prayer before a high school football game is not permissible. But spontaneous student-led prayers are acceptable.

Many public campuses permit an invocation at commencement or the start of the school year. Many college athletic programs encourage students to pray at the beginning of a game, with coaches often joining in. Courts seem to permit expression of faith if the students act on their own.

Student Fees: Support of Offensive Personal Beliefs. Students at the University of Wisconsin filed suit alleging that the university must grant them the choice not to fund registered student organizations that engage in political and ideological expression offensive to their personal beliefs. The Supreme Court decided the case in 2000 on free speech grounds, but the case is applicable to expression of religious or spiritual beliefs as well. The Court held that the First Amendment permits a public university to charge its students an activity fee used to fund programs to facilitate extracurricular student speech, provided the program is viewpoint-neutral. That is, so long as the program does not involve funding upon the basis of the subject matter of the program, students are required to pay the required activity fee. The Court noted that "if a university determines that its mission is well served if students have the means to engage in dynamic discussions on a broad range of issues, it may impose a mandatory fee to sustain such dialogue" (*Board of Regents of the University of Wisconsin System* v. *Southworth et al.,* 2000). This case gives student affairs staff the basis for providing support to a faith-based, spiritual organization, as long as it is done on neutral grounds. This requires that student activities staff work with student government funding sources to correctly implement the funding regulations of the particular campus.

Discussing Religious Beliefs in Class. A professor of exercise philosophy at the University of Alabama made occasional reference to his personal religious beliefs as part of his class lectures. The chair of the program directed the professor to refrain from making such comments. The professor filed suit, claiming the directive inhibited his right to free exercise of his religious beliefs and constituted an establishment of religion. The Eleventh Circuit Court of Appeals held that the directive neither violated the professor's exercise of religious beliefs nor established a religion. The court indicated that the ban on speaking about personal religious beliefs in class was directed to his teaching practices, which schools have authority to reasonably control as they control the content of the classroom (*Bishop* v. *Aronov*, 1991). This case enables student affairs staff to explore discussion of personal beliefs through their programs, such as leadership development workshops and courses, community service initiatives, and programming in housing that uses the wellness model.

Student Activity Fees Withheld from Student Organization. Campus Crusade for Christ, a student organization, sought funding from a university to sponsor a campuswide Bible study intended to reach out and inform students with the message of the gospel. The purpose of the program was to assist students in dealing with relationships from a Christian point of view. The university's funding policy prohibited funding any sectarian program of a university-recognized organization. To receive funding, the request must be for (1) a secular purpose, (2) neither advance nor inhibit religion, and (3) avoid excessive entanglement with religion.

The U.S. Ninth Circuit Court indicated that campuses have wide latitude in adopting funding policies to limited funds available to student organizations. In this case, the court held that there was no violation of the establishment clause as the funding policy complied with the requirements of *Lemon* v. *Kurtzman* (*Tipton* v. *University of Hawaii*, 1994). In cases such as this, a campus can establish reasonable parameters for funding student organizations. It may however, seek to increase the level of discussion of faith and spirit by adopting policies that permit funding of groups that explore questions nondenominationally.

Employment: Hiring. May an institution that is redrafting its application forms inquire as to an applicant's religious affiliation during the application process? In addressing these or similar situations, we must first ask whether the college is a public or private institution. The applicable law of the First Amendment or the Civil Rights Act may then be accurately identified. For instance, it would be difficult to argue effectively that a public institution has a legitimate nondiscriminatory reason for inquiring regarding the religious affiliation of an applicant. Some may argue that this is necessary for reasons of diversity, but it is difficult to imagine that such a position would be successful in the courts. However, if the institution is private, the question on the institution's application forms may be permitted.

In terms of employment, sectarian schools may embrace the traditions of a denomination, thereby creating a legitimate concern that to remain sectarian in nature a percentage of the employees of the institution must be members in good standing of a particular denomination. This may be the case at, say, the University of Notre Dame, Brigham Young University, or Yeshiva University. However, such institutions are legally required not to discriminate in hiring others of a different faith. In student affairs divisions on these campuses, open discussion of faith is commonplace. Staff are encouraged or may be required as part of their jobs to foster the faith development of students. Staff need to consider this aspect of their roles in conjunction with their own personal beliefs and practices.

Employment and Students: Observance of Sabbath Days. May a college require an employee to work on the Sabbath day of the employee's religion? May a faculty member refuse to reschedule an exam that is scheduled to be given on a day that one student indicates is his or her Sabbath? Would requiring the employee to work and the student to complete the exam on the Sabbath day violate free exercise of religion that is protected under both the First Amendment and the Civil Rights Act?

In applying the principles of the First Amendment and the Civil Rights Act, courts and government agencies acknowledge that these principles are not absolute. That is, they require that employers and colleges "reasonably accommodate" the religious beliefs and practices of employees and students. Resolving the question then requires examining the accommodations that can be made under the particular circumstances. For instance, in the leading case of *TWA, Inc.* v. *Hardison* (1977), an employee was called in to work for another employee on Saturday, his Sabbath day and one on which he was not scheduled to work. When the employee refused, TWA was required to bring in another employee, in violation of its seniority system and at substantially higher pay. The court held that this was unreasonable, and that termination of the employee who refused to work because of his Sabbath day was justified. This case appears extreme, given higher education's leading role in creating a diverse work environment respectful of religious as well as other differences. It would be highly unlikely for a college to terminate an employee for not working on a religious holiday. Similarly, reasonable accommodations are normally made for a student's request to change the day of an exam for religious reasons.

Use of Campus Facilities. Should the director of the student union grant a request by a group of students for space in the union for a Bible study group? This is an issue perhaps more sensitive for secular institutions than for private ones. The Supreme Court has clearly permitted state-operated colleges to give equal access to groups even though there is a religious or spiritual purpose to the meeting as long as the policies in allowing campus space are neutral as to religion. For instance, in *Widmar* v. *Vincent* (1981) the Supreme Court was presented with the question of whether the policy of the University of Missouri, Kansas City, that permitted student organizations to use campus facilities for political, cultural, educational, social, and recreation events but prohibited use for religious worship service or teaching violated the First Amendment. The Court concluded that such a policy did violate the First Amendment as it served to deny religious groups equal access to campus facilities.

A similar result was reached when University of Delaware students were denied use of a commons room of a residence hall for the purpose of religious services. The state supreme court held such a prohibition to be a violation of the students' right to free exercise of their religion (*Keegan v. Delaware*, 1974). The Constitution requires governments to treat religion and spirituality neutrally and the same when individuals and groups are similarly situated. Private colleges (which are not subject to constitutional limitations, only statutory ones) generally are free to assign space on campus. These cases present examples of how student affairs staff can assist students in exercising their faith within the campus community. This not only benefits the individual(s) involved but also exposes others to alternative faith beliefs and practices—something desirable for a liberal arts education and a well-rounded individual.

Student Housing. A group of Orthodox Jewish students claimed that a sexually free atmosphere of a college's required residential housing offended their religious traditions. May they be exempted from the campus housing requirement?

Indicating that "the students . . . . do not allege any facts from which a discriminatory intent could be inferred, do not argue that the [college] had a discriminatory intent, and, in fact, describe the [college's] motive as economic," the U.S. Second Circuit Court denied the students' claim under the Fair Housing Act (*Chronicle of Higher Education—Today's News,* 2001). This case shows that although campuses must not discriminate against students on the basis of religion, they also can expect reasonable policy to be upheld by the courts. Colleges cannot be expected to alter campus culture to fit the dictates of each religion.

Display of Religious Symbols. May a faculty member display in his or her office a religious symbol in the face of a student's complaint that such a symbol is offensive given the student's religious affiliation? This scenario presents a real clash between the free-exercise rights of an employee and the perspective of a student who does not want establishment of any particular religion on campus. Whether the institution is private or public, an opportunity exists for teaching about diversity of spiritual expression in the workplace.

Traditionally, display of religious symbols by the state or its employees in the course of their duties would not be permitted, as a violation of the establishment clause. However, the issue becomes more complex when the display is a mixture of clearly spiritual symbols with other symbols. As I suggested ear-

lier, the Supreme Court has addressed this issue in a nonschool setting dealing with government displays of crèches, Santa Claus and reindeer, meno-
rahs, and Christmas trees. In cases from Rhode Island and Pennsylvania, the
Court faced the question of allowing mixed displays on government property. In the Rhode Island case, the City of Cranston displayed a crèche with
a Santa Claus and reindeer. In the Pennsylvania case, Allegheny County displayed in its courthouse a menorah with a Christmas tree.

In deciding these cases, the Court stated that our culture is clearly one
that has a significant spiritual element. This is exemplified by the statement
"In God We Trust" appearing on our currency and on government buildings, among other places. Our Pledge of Allegiance makes reference to this
nation "under God." In addition, sessions of Congress and the courts are
opened with a prayer or invocation, often by a member of the clergy. These
displays are permissible and consistent with the First Amendment if the cultural aspect of the display is predominant. Presumably, this test would be
satisfied if the Santa Claus or Christmas tree were larger than the crèche or
menorah. Many of our college campuses have combined displays around
the December holidays incorporating numerous religious and secular symbols. The courts appear to favor a display where the cultural significance of
the symbols affords meaning and some learning. In addition, staff should
be able to display symbols of cultural significance of holidays they celebrate,
including those of a religious nature.

Conclusion

The purpose of this chapter has been to address the legal principles that
serve to support expression of religious or spiritual beliefs on a college and
university campus, as well as to examine the limitations imposed on such
expression. The chapter discussed the provisions of the U.S. Constitution,
the Civil Rights Act, and several relevant cases that apply in these areas.
These principles and cases tend to suggest that the law supports expression
of spirituality on a college campus through spontaneous expression of
prayer by a college student, equal access to campus facilities, invocations
and benediction at college ceremonies, displays of religious symbols as part
of a predominantly cultural display, reasonable accommodation of employee
and student Sabbath days, and spontaneous student-led prayer in the context of a high school or elementary school ceremony or sporting event.

The law tends not to support expression of spirituality through funding
religious groups on campus whose purpose is to evangelize, through a professor's inclusion of his or her personal religious beliefs as part of a course
lecture, or elementary and high school or elementary-school-sponsored
prayer relating to school ceremonies and sporting events.

The examples given here indicate that student affairs professionals are
situated uniquely to facilitate the learning process of body, mind, and spirit.
Student affairs staff can assist students in their development as whole persons

through many programs and services their departments sponsor. We encourage full discussion of the limits and exercise of expression on our campuses to enable staff to be aware of the legal issues—and, most important, their role in this area.

References

Astin, H., and Antonio, A. L. "Building Character in College." *About Campus,* Nov.–Dec. 2000.

Bishop v. *Aronov,* 926 F2d 1066 C. A. 11 (Ala.) (1991).

Board of Regents of the University of Wisconsin System v. *Southworth, et al.,* 529 U.S. 217, Mar. 22, 2000.

Chronicle of Higher Education—Today's News. "Federal Appeals Panel Rejects Orthodox Jews' Challenge of Yale's Housing Policy." January 4, 2001.

Keegan v. *Delaware,* 99 A. 2d 111, 1974.

Lee v. *Weisman,* 112. S. Ct., 1992.

Lemon v. *Kurtzman,* 403 USl 602, 1971.

McMurtrie, B. "College Will Apologize to Islamic Student Who Was Told Not to Pray Aloud in Class." *Chronicle of Higher Education—Today's News,* Jan. 5, 2000.

Palmer, P. "The Grace of Great Things: Reclaiming the Sacred in Knowing, Teaching and Learning." *The Sun,* Sep. 1998.

Smith v. *Board of Governors of North Carolina,* 429 F. Supp. 871 D.C. N.C. (1977).

Tipton v. *University of Hawaii,* 15 F 2d 922, 1994.

TWA, Inc. v. *Hardison,* 432 U.S. 63, 1977.

Widmar v. *Vincent,* 102 S. Ct. 269, 1981.

R. THOMAS CLARK *is the assistant dean for judicial affairs at the College of the Holy Cross, Worcester, Massachusetts.*

5

This chapter presents an overview of ideas for staff development that incorporate a spiritual dimension. Various aspects of professional practice are explored.

The Role of Spirituality in Student Affairs and Staff Development

Kathleen E. Allen, Gar E. Kellom

If there is one good reason to consider the spiritual development of student affairs staff, it is that it helps us survive personally and professionally in the demanding jobs we have. By the nature of our work and its responsibilities, we often put the concerns of students and other colleagues ahead of our own and regularly flirt with physical and emotional exhaustion. We owe it to ourselves to be grounded and centered, especially in the most challenging times of each semester, so we can speak and act from our core values. Walking the talk of our field and of our colleges is a way of professional life; for those of us working at a religiously affiliated institution, this also means integrating the values of our institution into our lives in a way that is meaningful to us.

We are managers and supervisors who have arrived at a position of influence with responsibility for training and retaining our personnel. The precious budget dollars in the professional development line items are a critical way in which we can offer meaningful staff meetings and workshops to boost productivity. Those goals cannot be accomplished without consideration of the whole person when working with staff. There is no more central part of the whole person than the spirit.

We are also mentors for students and for student paraprofessionals. We try to model holistic development, or integrated liberal arts, or character development that includes a spiritual dimension. Most often, we work through our staff to achieve these ends, but the ultimate goal is assessment of student growth on all dimensions. Our boards and the public demand nothing less.

You may not be reading this article for these reasons, however, but because of a yearning for greater aspiration and higher standards for your work. In the end, we are meaning makers. We structure the reality of college life through our programs, activities, and social-norming approaches. We want to create a better learning environment or learning community to prepare our students to assume leadership positions as good citizens in society. We hope to prepare students to speak to the deepest needs of those communities and start a snowball rolling in the direction of the common good because it is the right thing to do.

We seek nothing less than building a better world. We seek to change our institution into more than just an organization, to have the institution create an impact in higher education and for higher education to play a leadership role in building a better world. Our expectations of our staff members and their expectations of themselves are therefore high.

How do we devise a professional development program to speak to this level, to the deepest hopes and aspirations of our staff members? How do we prepare meaning makers for this type of social architecture? Preparing staff members for this challenge requires exploring the core values staff members hold dear, and understanding the core values of our institution.

When we talk of spiritual development, we are not speaking of "religiosity." This is a term referring to institutionalized religion or belonging to an established religious organization. We are speaking of the "spiritual dimension of a person's life," or that part of the holistic approach to student development and staff development. We see spiritual growth as the core dimension of a person's development, the key to further growth. Physical, emotional, psychological, social, environmental, and intellectual development are inextricably tied to spiritual growth and enhanced by paying attention to this as a vital component of learning.

Robert Bellah and colleagues (1985) have referred to this dimension as developing the "habits of the heart." This article is about developing habits of the heart in our staff members. We also examine the role that student affairs staff play in developing habits of the heart for our colleges and universities.

Where to begin? The starting point for enhancing the spiritual development of our student development staff is our own deep soul work, reflection on our own life and what gives it meaning. What is it that matters to us? What are the values that guide our life? Are there significant experiences that made us into the people we have become? How does what we believe influence our relationships with those who are close to us or those we work with? What has drawn us to the work we do? These and other questions can lead us into our soul work and enhance our own habits of the heart.

It is our experience in working with staff that they are willing to talk about their own spiritual journeys and what gives their lives meaning. We have yet to work with a group of student development professionals who were not on some level eager to share what was most important to them. As student affairs professionals, we have a unique opportunity and responsibility not only to foster the growth and development of the individual students and staff for which we are responsible (as well as our own) but also to affect the larger college environment. In short, we have the opportunity to create a better world locally on campus. To create that world requires positive action, but it also entails awareness of the pitfalls and roadblocks that await us.

Current Inhibitors to Soul Work in Student Affairs

Remember the ride at the amusement park in which when we enter the center of a large cylinder, which then starts to spin? The spinning increases until one by one we are pulled away from the center to the outer edge of the walls. At its peak speed, the floor drops out from under us, and we stay plastered against the outer wall.

This image is an analogy of the kind of work life that most of us experience in student affairs. We spin faster and faster, and eventually we can no longer hold onto the center. Over time, we are pulled apart from one another as the speed of "to dos" increases. Eventually the floor drops out from beneath us. Needless to say, it is difficult to live an examined life, if one is without a solid grounding.

Spiritual principles flow from the belief that we are all connected. This connectivity recognizes that we have an interdependent relationship with each other, and with all of nature. Juxtapose this idea with the fragmentation of our work lives. Despite the larger trend to blur boundaries, silos are still alive and well in higher education. Our language is one indicator of the boundaries we maintain. We use department and division names to mark our territory. We have informal rules of behavior that proclaim we should mind our own business ("I won't interfere in your work if you don't tell me what to do"). There also are subtle forms of power that keep us in our own space and don't support individuals who try to work across boundaries. For example, how many of us have seen or created a job description that is impossible for one person to accomplish? Or have a job that is bigger than a forty-hour work week?

The pressure to perform, please, and quickly complete our job tasks keeps us from living in the present. We put our heads down and plow through, which causes us not to be present to others and ourselves or develop the relationships necessary for facilitating connection. The pace of our work does not allow reflection. The action bias is strong in student affairs. We often define our worth on how fast we solve problems, or our ability to make problems go away. This creates a treadmill effect that works against reflective questioning and covenantal relationships.

Another cultural artifact of student affairs is the need for approval. This works against our own spiritual process. When we seek approval, we need to control those below us to create the conditions favoring approval by our boss. Controlling others diminishes their spiritual development and our own as well.

In student affairs, we not only have silos but also legal standards. The fear of being sued can cause us to be cautious and reduce our relationships to a transactional level. Spiritual relationships are formed in a covenant between people. A covenantal relationship extends beyond the legal minimum requirements. If we hold back or relate solely on the basis of legal standards, we also limit the quality and potential impact of our relationships. We learn to protect our organizations and ourselves, which eventually diminishes the service and care of our students and ourselves.

Two levels of support are needed to enhance the spirituality of our work in an organization. The first is organizational, the second individual. This section identifies ways to shape an organizational culture that reflects spiritual principles. The next section shares strategies for staff development that focus on enhancing an individual's spiritual journey and the collective spiritual development of staff.

Strategies for Shaping an Organizational Culture

So far, we have described the role of soul work in developing spirituality and how the student affairs culture hinders development of our staffs' spiritual lives. If we are to create a living community that supports spiritual practice and development, we need to shift our culture from one of a fragmented treadmill to one that encourages reflection, caring, community, and integration. The concepts or strategies presented here help develop a culture in student affairs that supports a living community. When we use the term *living community,* we define it as a place that gives energy instead of draining it. It fulfills and sustains the life of the group itself, and the members in it. The members of a living community recognize and act on the principle of interdependence and treat each other as sacred.

An Environment of Safety. If people don't feel safe at work, they don't reveal themselves. Over time, this diminishes their spiritual development, authenticity, and integrity. In *Leadership and Spirit* (2000), Russ Moxley discusses the role of collusion and its negative impact on an individual's spiritual development. He believes that control-based hierarchies arise from the unexamined emotional issues of positional managers. If managers are driven by approval, fear, insecurity, or anger, they are controlling of people who report to them. For example, if a vice president is worried about gaining the approval of the president, he or she needs to control the outcomes and behaviors of staff to deliver what the president wants. The impact of this behavior is to trigger another dynamic between staff and the VP. If they don't feel it is safe to disagree, they have to choose between collusion and commitment. If they collude, they say yes when they really want to say no, or remain silent when they want to speak their minds. When staff members choose collusion over commitment to their own authenticity and the institution's mission, their spirits are diminished. Therefore, it is important to create a culture of safety within student affairs and influence the larger institution to do the same.

Design Reasonable Jobs. Many organizations today, including student affairs, design job descriptions that are impossible for one person to do. Overloading a job description has negative implications for spiritual development of staff members. Having a job no one individual can complete adds to the frenetic doingness of our work lives. Spiritual development needs time for reflection and being, not just doing. A good place to start is with job descriptions that are doable and have expectations for reflection built in.

Develop Spiritual "Smoke Alarms." When we are so overworked that we become burned out, we cannot be present to each other. Signs of burnout among staff are a symptom of a larger problem in the culture of the organization. A living community has mechanisms to help people who need additional support get their jobs done or work through life's challenges. Employee assistance programs can give this support, or the help can come from colleagues who show concern or step in to help accomplish a task. Other organizations actually use burnout as a badge of quality in performance, an opportunity to pile more work on the individual, or even to take advantage of the weaknesses that show up under stress.

Organizations that pay attention to early warnings of burnout can intervene in a helpful and life supporting way. One director's staff group decided to become the means of support for each other by watching for early signs of overwork. Sharing their perceptions with each other, they offered encouragement and permission to change behavior.

Student affairs practitioners also need to examine their metaphors for work. For example, one dean of students thought of September as the start of a marathon that ended with graduation the following spring. Our metaphors can shape our own expectations of what life is supposed to be like; they often conflict with our spiritual journeys.

Shift Criteria for Performance Appraisal. Many of our performance reviews ask us to identify what we have accomplished. The assumption behind this form is that the more you can list, the higher you are rated. Shifting the criteria we use for evaluations can leverage change in your organization's culture. Criteria that support spiritual development for staff members include assessing one's personal development, developing reflective practices, and creating authenticity in relationships.

Treat Others As Sacred. What would happen if we treated each other as worthy of reverence and respect and we were willing to show appreciation and consideration to others? How would this change what we talk about, how we interact, and what we believe about each other? Today, the "lean and mean" organizational paradigm leaves little room for treating each other as sacred. If, conversely, we choose to set a new standard of sacredness for our relationships, we create a culture that supports the spiritual development of our staff. Something wonderful happens when we recognize the strengths and unique gifts in each other. We begin to reveal, instead of protect, ourselves. Our egos may then take a back seat, and we become open and receptive to change, ideas, suggestions, and appreciation.

Pay attention to what you do; become more intentional in your actions. Your behavior affects those around you, especially if you are in a position of leadership. If you hold a management position, you are metaphorically in the spotlight for your employees. Others watch you closely and use your actions as justification for their own behavior. A leader's behavior elicits responses in others and affects the environment of an organization. When a manager behaves with integrity and authenticity, others are given permission to be authentic as well. The modeling of the leader helps to create a climate of honesty and integrity within the organization. Being trusting and trustworthy invites others to trust in return. This allows people to talk frankly with each other and helps develop authenticity and integrity. If we are present to others, they feel appreciated. If a leader displays humor and enjoyment, it allows others to see humor in their own behavior. Laughter opens people up to positive feelings and can diminish judgment and negative feelings.

Strategies for Staff Development

Shaping organizational culture can be enhanced through staff development. It is the leader's role to facilitate opportunity for staff development and to change its paradigm. Here are ways leaders can be helped in facilitating the spiritual development of their staff. These suggestions are not designed to be complete; we expect that as you read and experiment with spiritual staff development activities, new and innovative ideas will emerge.

Centering Before a Staff Meeting. People often come into staff meetings with the thoughts and tasks they have left behind. This foreground keeps them from focusing on the present, each other, and the larger topics that form connections. Centering is a technique that helps people let go of their foreground and focus on the meeting. In some ways, it allows our various molecules to catch up with rapid movement from our individual offices to the staff meeting. Centering can come in the form of quiet, a reading, a prayer, or storytelling.

Reading Group. An informal reading group using spiritual books and articles can give staff members the opportunity to delve deeply into their own spiritual journey. Such a group brings together people who can then carry on exploration with a structured reading. They choose the amount of reading required for each session and leave some time to discuss their individual insights, questions, or different reactions. Groups often meet over lunch or breakfast.

Busy Person's Retreat. This is an individually structured week where a staff member agrees to take three thirty-minute breaks each day for meditation, spiritual guidance, and quiet. The length of the retreat can vary, but usually a one-week time frame is used. The concept of using a retreat to further spiritual growth is found in various monastic traditions. The breaks in a week enable you to slow down, take time to reflect on your life, and be nurtured in your own spiritual journey. This can be life-changing. One student affairs staff development program used the busy person's retreat annually each January. The campus ministry office, in cooperation with a local monastery, organized the program. Each person spent thirty minutes in meditation or prayer, at his or her choice. The next thirty minutes were spent sharing prayers with the sisters, and the third thirty-minute time block was spent talking with a spiritual guide or director. The staff members who experienced this program said that it gave them a new perspective on their job and their lives. They were also able to be more present to their students and colleagues.

Celebration. Celebration and ritual have a long tradition in religious organizations. As student affairs practitioners, we are often in the role of maintaining or initiating celebrations for students. However, we rarely see ourselves as one of the constituents for whom we should plan celebrations. They create a breathing space to enjoy the present and focus on our strengths. They often give us hope and strength for the challenging times ahead.

Sabbatical or Administrative Leave. Most spiritual traditions have a practice of going on a journey or pilgrimage to deepen faith development. In higher education, we have the practice of the sabbatical for faculty (and sometimes for administrative staff). Taking advantage of this time-out has a positive effect on a person's spiritual growth. When we shift our pace to one of reflection, following a passion or researching an interest can have residual spiritual impact on our lives.

Retreat. Many student affairs organizations have retreats for all or some of their staff. Retreats are too often just another form of a meeting, only longer. We overload an agenda with too many topics and issues that need attention, too many decisions to be made. However, a retreat can also be a powerful vehicle in support of spiritual development. When we use retreats for this purpose, we include time for reflection, fun, and celebration.

Reflection Time. In student affairs, our cultural bias is one of action; we are often judged institutionally (as well as justifying our value to others) on how much we do. Therefore, giving permission and creating a space for reflection can make a counterculture statement that the organization values being as well as doing. One campus has a reflection room in the student center where staff, faculty, and students can go to be quiet. Another organization created interruption-free time zones of two hours per week for all staff. During these times, staff members cannot schedule meetings, take calls, or answer e-mail. They use the time to think, reflect, and spontaneously visit and build relationships with each other. This creates small patches of slow time where internal stimulation and integration can be supported and achieved.

Staff Service Days. Having staff participate as a group in service activity in the community reminds us that we are related to people beyond the campus. One's spiritual life can be nurtured by serving others. Not only does it set a good example to our students; it brings spiritual principles into visible action. Such projects as Habitat for Humanity or "urban plunge" allow a social justice orientation to evolve for our staff and ourselves.

Outdoor Experiences. Many people experience the outdoors as a spiritual dimension. When we hike a mountain together, canoe down a river, or sit side by side at a campfire, we use the natural spiritual connection of the activity to enhance our own connection with each other, nature, and our spirits.

How Enhancing the Spiritual Capacity of Staff Affects Student Development

Through cultivating the spiritual growth of each student affairs staff person, individuals become stronger and more centered, speaking and acting from core values. These voices of authenticity raise the conversation above the level of everyday management headaches that tend to bog us down in details and cause us to forget the reasons we went into this work to begin with. The individual voices of authenticity can become a chorus creating a pocket of energy within our division, attracting others who want to stay connected to the importance of student affairs work.

In creating healthier, happier staff members connected to their highest ideals, we also transform our division. As individuals find their souls and do their own soul work, our division is enhanced from the inside out. As the individual staff person becomes more fulfilled and productive through spiritual growth, the division is enhanced. It is a pocket of positive energy within the institution that students, faculty, and other staff are attracted to. Partnerships are formed, relationships are enhanced, and collaboration is fostered.

Tapping into the values and aspirations of our staff enables communication among others who have a similar hope of building a better learning environment for students. The goal of working across departmental boundaries is easier to achieve because there is a stronger bridge to span the boundaries. As a result, student affairs becomes a respected part of the institution, called upon with greater frequency to offer leadership on key institutional objectives. The sense of worth of the staff is enhanced, as is the reputation of and respect for the division.

Peter Senge (1994) has said that an institution cannot go where its employees do not want to go. This is leadership through values. Connecting individuals to their own core values and to the core values of the institution creates a common ground. In an organizational culture supportive of the spiritual journey of the individual, the growth of the organization is also enhanced.

You might say that as student development staff develop their own habits of the heart, they also nurture the heart of the institution. We are the ones called upon to interpret the mission of the institution in the midst of a campus crisis attracting media attention. In those times, the real values of the college or university become clear. We are often asked to make sense of an institutional policy decision that has packed a student government meeting or made headlines in the student paper. We are the architects of the organizational culture in the residence halls, athletic departments, and student organizations. We may be the custodians of the collective soul of the campus.

As faculty seek to create for students a life of the mind that fosters discussion, critical thinking, and the ability to communicate, student affairs staff are in key positions to nurture the habits of the heart of the institution. Through professional development, we can offer staff some grounding in the value of their own spiritual development. Then our staff members grow and develop; our division of student affairs is enhanced; and our institution becomes a stronger, more open, and more caring place.

References

Bellah, R., and others. *Habits of the Heart.* Los Angeles: University of California Press, 1985.

Moxley, R. *Leadership and Spirit: Breathing New Vitality and Energy into Individuals and Organizations.* San Francisco: Jossey-Bass, 2000.

Senge, P. *Fifth Discipline Fieldbook: Strategies and Tools for Building a Learning Organization.* New York: Doubleday, 1994.

KATHLEEN E. ALLEN *is a former vice president for student affairs and consults widely on organizational change, leadership, and spirituality.*

GAR E. KELLOM *is the vice president of student development at St. John's University, Minnesota.*

6

The role of spirituality in graduate preparation programs is explored, with suggestions offered for improving the experience for students in education.

Spiritual Dimensions of Graduate Preparation in Student Affairs

C. Carney Strange

For many individuals, the decision to pursue graduate studies signals a recommitment of some sort—whether to capitalize on previous educational success, explore a newly discovered interest, change directions from a career that has lost its meaning, or simply continue a transition not yet completed. For those who pursue student affairs graduate preparation in particular, such motives betray myriad reasons for what they seek. Familiar to us are the archetypes of undergraduate student leader, the superinvolved joiner, or the resident assistant extraordinaire who sets sights on a graduate degree in this field. For some, this is a profession they have long courted; for others, at the eleventh hour, this is a discovery of an opportunity they never previously considered and didn't even know existed. There is also the career changer who appears at our office door to talk about how unfulfilling the first few years in a chosen field have been. Finally, there are those who are continuing a developmental process they are not ready to close in entering adult life.

Regardless of the particulars of the journey, what appears common to all these candidates is their experience of a significant life transition. Levinson and Levinson (1996) portrayed transition to be unstable and full of questions, as individuals terminate their current life structure, make choices about what aspects to let go, and initiate a life structure for the purpose of moving on to a new period of stability. In the case of many of our graduate students, this is the early-adult life phase.

NEW DIRECTIONS FOR STUDENT SERVICES, no. 95, Fall 2001   © John Wiley & Sons, Inc.

A period of transition is marked by familiar affective courses, vacillating between a sense of loss for what was thought to be secure and the excitement of new possibilities. So it may be with the graduate school experience, when many students transform the sense of uncertainty accompanying a departure from one life structure (say, undergraduate leader) to a sense of confidence accompanying another (entering a new profession). Inherent in this process may be what Parks (2000) identifies as the timely emergence in their lives of "big questions" and "worthy dreams."

Indeed, enrollment in graduate studies often legitimizes such concerns in people's lives. Under the protection and structure of an academic program, questions such as "Who am I?" and "Where am I going?" form a powerful personal discourse, while mentors engage in advising, peers encounter one another, and course credits fulfill degree and certificate requirements. Choices abound and resources are plentiful for exploration as the nervous conjecture of those who stand by in a supportive role (parent, spouse, friend, significant other) is soon quieted in the simple recognition that "she's in grad school."

All of this is to say that for most the graduate school experience is a time of personal inventory and significant change, not unlike other periods of transition in life when fundamentals of self identity, relationship with others, and ultimate direction are open to examination and reformation. Such considerations have long served the purposes of higher learning but only now are beginning to reappear in our discussion in more resolute form under the rubric of authenticity, faith, and spirituality (Astin, 1999; Love and Talbot, 1999; Palmer, 1998; Parks, 2000; Strange, 2000).

Understanding Spirituality

Spirituality is interpreted variously, depending on concerns, expectations, and experiences. For many, the spiritual domain is equated with a specific religious tradition or practice; for some, spirituality is a private experience of connection to some unifying and universal presence; and for others, it is tantamount to a profound sentiment of peace and contentment. Discussion of these matters usually touches upon aspects of many perspectives, a point that renders consideration of the topic complex and problematic. For purposes of our discussion, there are several defining characteristics that have emerged in the literature recently that may prove helpful in sharpening our focus.

McColman (1997) noted that spirituality is rooted in the classical Latin derivative *spiritus* (and similarly in Greek and Hebrew), meaning "breath" or "to breathe." In essence, spirituality refers to that which makes one breathe, or to that in life worth breathing for. Fowler equates spirituality, or faith, with the capacity to actively intuit "life as a whole" through relatedness among self, other, and some "center of value and power" (1981, p. 17). Parks emphasizes "faithing" as a human activity entailing the ongoing "seeking and discovering [of] meaning in the most comprehensive dimensions of our experience" (2000, p. 7). This ongoing meaning making "frames, colors, provides tone and texture, and relativizes the activity of the everyday. All human action is conditioned by a felt sense of how life really is (or ought to be), or what has ultimate value" (p. 21). It involves "putting one's heart upon that which one trusts as true. It is a bedrock trust that the pattern one sees is real . . . the ongoing composing of the heart's true resting place" (p. 24).

Zohar and Marshall (2000) also equate the domain of spirituality to the fundamental human concerns of meaning making: "The search for meaning is evident in so many aspects of our lives. What is my life all about? What does my job mean? the company I have founded or work for? this relationship? Why am I studying for this degree? What does it mean to be me? What does it mean that I am going to die some day? Why commit myself to one thing or another, to one person or another—or to anything?" (p. 20).

Although some are uncomfortable with the parlance of spirituality (faith, belief, soul, God), the essence of this discourse seems to focus on the importance and role of a meaningful center in one's life upon which to ground a sense of ultimate purpose and direction. Whether regarded as spiritual in nature or otherwise, such questions frequently coincide in people's lives with pursuit of advanced formal education. In that sense, these are concerns that mark the journey of every graduate student, as new directions are explored in light of life's broadest dimensions. For some, these dimensions are manifest in questions of self-definition and understanding: What inspires me? What are my hopes and fears? Of what value am I? For others, they are concerns of a relational kind: To whom am I attached? Where is my community? How do I experience love? forgiveness? For most, they are queries about ultimate goals: What compels me in life? Whom do I serve? For what would I be willing to give my life?

Zohar and Marshall (2000) suggest that those most capable of addressing such concerns are distinguished by advanced levels of "spiritual intelligence" (p. 15), a dimension they describe in terms of certain capacities and qualities (being flexible and self-aware, having the capacity to face and use suffering, being inspired by vision and values, being reluctant to cause unnecessary harm, and tending to see connection between diverse things and to ask *Why?* or *What if?*—while seeking fundamental answers). According to those authors, such qualities constitute a spiritual quotient (*SQ*, complementary to other forms of intelligence) that is called upon "when we need to be flexible, visionary or creatively spontaneous" (pp. 13–14). In their analysis, it is our primary tool for addressing "existential problems— problems where we feel personally stuck, trapped by our own past habits or neuroses or problems with illness and grief. SQ makes us aware that we have existential problems, and it enables us to solve them—or at least to find peace about them. It gives us a 'deep' sense of what life's struggles are about" (pp. 13–14).

These various discussions of spirituality seem to coalesce around the importance of life's broadest dimensions in orienting and inspiring individuals with regard to their sense of purpose, direction, efficacy, and connection to others. Given the observation that these concerns of a spiritual kind, as defined here, accompany the challenges, tasks, and commitments of the graduate school experience, it follows that advanced education presents an important opportunity for students and programs alike to address this domain.

Spirituality and Higher Education

From its inception, American higher education has long honored a relationship between the intellectual and the spiritual. Particularly in the beginning, education of the whole person—knowledge, talents, body, soul, and character—guided the enterprise, and questions of the ultimate formed the discourse of the day. However, in the ensuing period postsecondary education has witnessed a distinct dividing of the waters, with things of the spirit receding to one bank and those of the intellect to the other. What was once a familiar conversation to most members of the academy has now become a disjointed discussion, as attention to the human spirit has all but faded from the landscape of liberal learning.

This is perhaps even more so the case for graduate education, where success for students and faculty alike increasingly has become dependent on a great degree of specialization and expertise at the expense of integration and synthesis of understanding. Consequently, at the graduate level the authentic, holistic, educational experience may be most in jeopardy. Such is the observation made here in the context of graduate preparation in student affairs. How can a broader view be restored, and how might faculty, department administrators, and graduate students contribute to its restoration? This analysis turns now to suggestions for how such ends might be served in the interest of student growth and development in student affairs graduate preparation.

Creating Learning Communities of Spirit

In a new edition of her previous work (Parks, 1986), Sharon Parks (2000) devotes attention to the kind of human environment thought to promote and encourage the meaning-making process she denotes as faithing, or for purposes of this discussion spirituality. In her analysis, these are "mentoring communities" that recognize, support, challenge, and inspire those within them. Her prescriptive criteria offer a helpful template for evaluating graduate departments and programs as an educational setting where the pursuit of meaning making in its broadest dimension and significance might occur. Such an environment can indeed nurture the spiritual questions in students' lives at a time when they are paramount.

Network of Belonging. The first criterion, a network of belonging, is an essential quality of any environment hopeful of making a difference in students' lives. It is the starting point from which a deep sense of security emerges, roles for involvement are discovered, and full membership in community is experienced, all conditions common to a powerful educational setting (Strange and Banning, 2001). According to Parks, "a mentoring community is a network of belonging that constitutes a spacious home for the potential and vulnerability of the young adult imagination in practical, tangible terms" (2000, p. 135). It serves both "to reassure and to encourage the development of inner-dependence" (p. 136). Although reflecting specifically on the experiences of traditional-age undergraduates, Parks makes comments that readily apply to more advanced students as well. A sense of belonging is requisite to any kind of engagement that challenges and inspires students at this juncture, and failure to achieve this condition jeopardizes the activities that lead to the active exploration and risk taking so essential to learning.

Numerous policies and practices can enhance this sense of belonging among students. From beginning to end, opportunities abound in graduate education to connect students to one another and to reaffirm their presence; rites and rituals are particularly potent in this regard. The combined effects of a well-designed orientation program, a ceremonial convocation, a picnic, and other social or informational gatherings can secure immediate feelings of attachment and welcome. Likewise, at the other end, a closing awards ceremony or recognition banquet, commencement, and other culminating exercises can seal the experience to remind graduates that they are always welcome to return to the place where their lives were changed, and where their imprint is visible. The spiritual journey of graduate studies must begin with a fundamental sense of belonging.

Big Enough Questions. Graduate school is inherently a time for questioning in students' lives. Beyond the usual critical reflection on the body of knowledge informing the field, students themselves are the source of many questions that extend from their own life experience and that sound once again in the midst of a life transition. Parks suggests that mentoring environments have the "capacity to extend hospitality to big questions" (2000, p. 137). Thus in addition to what it means to be an emerging professional in student affairs, students often grapple with other concerns of personal consequence: How does this career balance with other dimensions of my life? Are there trade-offs? Is work in higher education worth it? Can I commit my life to these institutions? Toward what ends are we moving in this field?

Other questions extend from the inevitable dilemmas and challenges of graduate internship and other hands-on experience: Can I live with the compromises I sometimes face in responding to students' needs? Where are my loyalties? How do I resolve inconsistencies I witness among those I admire most in this profession? What hypocrisies tarnish my own actions in that regard?

"Big questions," says Parks, "stretch us. They reveal the gaps in our knowledge, in our social arrangements, in our ambitions and aspirations.

Big questions are . . . ones that ultimately matter" (2000, p. 137). Whether immediate or long-term, the power of big questions must be attended to in the lives of graduate students. Advising relationships, mentoring systems, and capstone seminars all create opportunities during the graduate experience for revisiting such questions as they emerge and challenge dimensions of personal and professional identity, relationships, and purposes.

Encounters with Otherness. In a world characterized by increasing diversity, the importance of encounters with otherness in a mentoring community is perhaps self-evident. More obvious is the point that graduates who have little or no exposure to cultural differences simply won't fare as well in a global, pluralistic society. By contrast, less obvious is the point that a capacity for taking on big questions in life depends on exposure to diverse backgrounds and experiences. Parks notes that "one of the most significant features of the human adventure is the capacity to take the perspective of another and to be compelled thereby to recompose one's own perspective, one's own faith" (2000, p. 140).

As shifts occur in the context and circumstances that a diverse environment engenders, participants must reexamine their own commitment and understanding to discover broader connections than those previously considered. The challenge and gift of a diverse mentoring environment is that "an empathic bond is established that transcends us and them, creating a new we. This grounds commitment to the common good, rather than just to me and mine" (Parks, 2000, p. 139–140). This creates an encounter of relationship rather than agreement (Eck, 2000).

For those preparing for a career in student affairs, otherness comes in many forms. Whether by gender, race and ethnicity, sexual orientation, age, religious belief, disability, or institutional status and role (faculty, administrator, student), individual differences can form a rich humus for the graduate school experience (Strange and Alston, 1998), as long as "hospitality to otherness is prized and practiced" (Parks, 2000, p. 141). Encounters with differences are essential to the human vulnerability that promotes "consciousness of another, and thus [vulnerability] to reimagining self, other, world, and 'God'" (Parks, 2000, p. 141).

Habits of Mind. Mentoring environments also create "norms of discourse and inclusion that invite genuine dialogue, strengthen critical thought, encourage connective-holistic awareness, and develop the contemplative mind" (Parks, 2000, p. 142). If graduate education is about anything, it is most expressly about these habits of mind. Critique, connective thinking, and contemplation form the curricular core of program courses and assignments. Dialogue between faculty and students, or among peers, is at the heart of the matter in setting in motion the processes of meaning making that underlie spirituality.

"When one speaks," Parks observes, "and then is heard—but not quite, and therefore tries to speak yet more clearly—and then listens to the other—and understands, but not quite, and listens again—one becomes actively engaged in sorting out what is true and dependable within oneself and about one's world. How one makes meaning is composed and recomposed in this process" (p. 142). Development of critical thought also contributes to the goal: "One becomes a young adult in faith [or spirituality] when one can begin to reflect critically on one's own ways of making meaning at the level of ultimacy" (p. 143).

But skills of analysis, critique, and discrimination are only the beginnings of graduate work. Equally important is holistic thought, or "the capacity to discover fitting connections among things, to recognize how the vast tissue of life is dynamically and interdependently composed" (p. 144). It is out of these moments that "mentoring environments . . . welcome and encourage grappling with ways of seeing the whole of life" (p. 145). Finally, as insights do occur, mentoring environments initiate individuals "into the power of pause" (p. 145) or contemplation, that is, the opportunity to be in the silent presence of what one has come to terms with (if only temporarily) in regard to ultimate questions and purposes. Contemplation calls for times of quiet alertness to what has transpired.

Worthy Dreams. The Dream (Levinson and Levinson, 1996) forms the foundation for building one's life structure. A worthy dream constitutes "a quality of vision . . . an imagined possibility that orients meaning, purpose, and aspiration" (Parks, 2000, p. 146). In many ways, it is the pursuit of the dream that motivates and accompanies the decision of many students to pursue graduate work in the first place. Some come to explore an interest discovered while leading, serving, or participating with others as undergraduates. Some build on earlier commitment to a career path shared by admired others who have modeled for them the student affairs profession. For others, such a step represents the termination of a different dream once held but now realized as no longer worthy or attainable. Whatever the case, the graduate school experience is essentially an act of dreaming about one's purpose in life—in the most spiritual sense, one's calling or vocation. Parks (2000) speaks of this as "a relational sensibility in which I recognize that what I do with my time, talents, and treasure is most meaningfully conceived not as a matter of personal passion and preference but in relationship to the whole of life. . . . Vocation is the place where the heart's deep gladness meets the world's deep hunger" (Parks, 2000, p. 148, paraphrasing Friedrich Buechner's famous metaphor). A mentoring community gives rise to the opportunity to explore such questions. Why education? Why higher education? Why student affairs? Whom do I serve, and for what purpose? These are queries that go to the heart of an educator's call to this field.

Access to Images. A powerful mentoring environment is itself a community of imagination, offering "images of truth, transformation, positive images of self and of the other, and images of interrelatedness" (p. 148). These are images of truth that offer a complete picture, incorporating the "realities of suffering [as well as] the awe of wonder" (p. 151); they are images of transformation that distill a "hope for renewing the world"; they are affirming images of self "that convey a faithful correspondence between [one's] own aspirations and positive reflection in the eyes of another whom [one] values and trusts" (p. 151); they include "images of the other as both similar and unique" and "images of interrelatedness and wholeness" about "institutions that work" (p. 151).

The discourse of graduate education is rich with stories and images of truth and goodness, as well as failures. On the positive side, from the *Student Personnel Point of View* (American Council on Education, 1937) and *Pieces of Eight* (Appleton, Briggs, and Rhatigan, 1978) to *Involving Colleges* (Kuh and others, 1991) and *Good Practices* (Blimling and Whitt, 1999), student affairs graduate students have many opportunities to explore what it means to be an effective professional and how to design an effective institutional environment (Strange and Banning, 2001). It is out of these images that worthy dreams can evolve and be embraced.

Community of Practice

A mentoring environment also engages in the "practices of hearth, table, and commons" (Parks, 2000, p. 154). Hearth includes spaces where individuals are "warmed in both body and soul, are made comfortable, and tend to linger." Whether in faculty members' offices, department lounges, or favorite gathering sites, such places "invite pause, reflection, and conversation" (p. 154).

The practice of table works in a similar way. "In every culture, human beings have eaten together," Parks writes (p. 156). "The practice of the table prepares us for *civitas* . . . we learn to share, to wait, to accommodate, to be grateful. . . . we learn delayed gratification, belonging, commitment, and ritual" (p. 156). Above all, though, the table, like the hearth, is a place of dialogue and conversation, where dreams are shared and images are explored among peers and mentors.

Last, the practice of commons affords opportunities of "interrelatedness, belonging, and learning how to stand—and stand with—each other over time" (p. 156). Such places "confirm a common, connected life, and in common with various forms of story and ritual, it can become the center of shared faith and grounded hope" (p. 157). Perhaps they are "third places" (Oldenberg, 1989), where individuals can relax for an extended period of time, free from the stress of daily pressures and open to dialogue and deep conversation around life's large questions. For many, reflection on the graduate school experience almost always rekindles fond memories of places like these, where faculty and students gathered often and informally to critique ideas, hear good stories, enjoy spontaneous moments, solve world problems, and renew a sense of purpose and commitment to it all.

Thus, in summary, a powerful mentoring environment—whether in the workplace, in the family, a religious faith community, an institution of higher learning, or a graduate program—offers participants "a network of belonging, big enough questions, encounters with otherness, important habits of mind, worthy dreams, [and] access to key images, concepts (content), and practices . . . " (p. 135). These are the program conditions to which student affairs graduate educators must aspire if they are to serve the spiritual dimensions of their students' lives.

Conclusions and Recommendations

In response to the historical dominance of objectivism, competitive individualism, and a "culture of disconnection" in higher education, Palmer (1998) calls for creating "communities of truth" where creative conflict draws upon the knowledge of the group, protected by the "compassionate fabric of human caring itself" (Palmer, 1987, pp. 20–25). In such places, Palmer advocates exploring "the spiritual dimension of teaching, learning, and living" wherein occurs the "ancient and abiding human quest for connectedness with something larger and more trustworthy than our egos—with our own souls, with one another, with the worlds of history and nature, with the invisible winds of the spirit, with the mystery of being alive" (1998–99, p. 6). Love and Talbot have admonished student affairs professionals in particular to "be open to issues of spiritual development in students" (1999, p. 371). Perhaps this challenge dictates that we see our work as graduate educators differently, not so much as training professionals for a particular field as guiding individuals to discover their own sources of connectedness to something larger and more trustworthy in their lives.

Acknowledging the insight of the emerging epistemology—that "all knowing is inevitably also a valuing" (p. 163)—Parks (2000) contends that "the academy is by intention or default a community of imagination in recomposing knowledge and faith." Within such a community, each "syllabus functions as a professor's 'testimony,' as a 'confession of faith'. . . [insofar as it] declare[s] what they believe to be of value: questions, images, insights, concepts, theories, sources, and methods of inquiry that they have found to lead toward a worthy apprehension of truth" (p. 165).

In these analyses, it becomes clear that we all serve as spiritual guides whether by happenstance or conscious effort. It is inevitable, then, that in the same way we have found this field "to be a worthy place of investment," we stand in testimony to students as to our "own composing of meaning" (Parks, 2000, p. 165). It is therefore important that we individually and collectively profess our "intuitions, apprehensions, and convictions of truth, in a manner that encourages dialogue with the emerging inner authority of the student" (p. 167). We do this by "beckoning the spirit—the animating essence—of the student" (p. 167) and by bearing a "tradition, [while] participating with the student in [our] community's ongoing composing of wisdom" (p. 168). This requires both poetic imagination and passion, so "that the spirit of the student is beckoned out and finds fitting forms in which to dwell" (p. 169).

Responding to these challenges requires reaffirming some of what we currently do, perhaps creating new initiatives, and certainly becoming more intentional about those policies and practices that already serve such ends. Deep within the ethos of student affairs is a passion for the transformative power of learning. Our roots are embedded in the hope of a rational humanism that offers promise to anyone who is willing to change for the better. Our philosophy embraces differences and recognizes that the whole student indeed comes to school (ACE, 1937, 1949; NASPA, 1987). We are also partners in an enterprise that serves the broader society with values that are distinct and resolute (Young, 1997). Reaffirming the sense of mission that emanates from this legacy is an obvious step in the directions outlined here.

As for current policies and practices, it might be worth the effort of a program review committee, comprising faculty, students, and practicing professionals, to examine a graduate program's present features in light of these characteristics of the mentoring environment. Which practices invoke a sense of belonging? How does the program articulate its values? How do the curriculum and other program features attend to issues of diversity? Is there opportunity for reflection and retreat? What culminating experiences tie program components together? Do faculty share their own justifications, hopes, and fears for the field? for life in general? Are there program-gathering spaces? How do students and faculty come together? What collective opportunities are there for service to others?

Answers to such questions can deliver an agenda for a future program initiative as well. For example, concerns about the practice of table might lead to developing an annual banquet where program members gather to celebrate the year's accomplishments and to enjoy one another's company. Questions about encounters of otherness might result in a program implementing a "voice project" requirement (Strange and Alston, 1998) where attempts to reach across differences are integrated and ritualized in the curriculum. Finally, a program day of reflection, to focus on a common reading of professional import, might result from a commitment to strengthen opportunities for contemplation and worthy dreaming.

All such initiatives are geared toward raising what Parks calls "a consciousness of the commons," a calling to work "on behalf of our common life" (2000, pp. 174–175). As this "central strength of the professions" (pp. 174–175) is exercised, our students begin to realize that the "work of the head, the heart, and the hand is transformed into a larger consciousness, into new ways of seeing, being, knowing, and acting in the world" (p. 178). This is indeed a worthy goal.

References

American Council on Education. *The Student Personnel Point of View.* (American Council on Education Studies, series 1, no. 3.) Washington, D.C.: American Council on Education, 1937.

American Council on Education, Committee on Student Personnel Work. (E. G. Williamson, chair). *The Student Personnel Point of View.* (Rev. ed.; American Council on Education Studies, series 6, no. 13.) Washington, D.C.: American Council on Education, 1949.

Appleton, J., Briggs, C., and Rhatigan, J. *Pieces of Eight: The Rites, Roles, and Styles of the Dean by Eight Who Have Been There.* Portland, Oreg.: NASPA Institute of Research and Development, 1978.

Astin, A., and Astin, H. *Meaning and Spirituality in the Lives of College Faculty: A Study of Values, Authenticity, and Stress.* Los Angeles: University of California, Higher Education Research Institute. 1999

Blimling, G., and Whitt, E. *Good Practices in Student Affairs: Principles to Foster Student Learning.* San Francisco: Jossey-Bass, 1999.

Eck, D. "A Snapshot of Religious America." *Spirituality and Health,* Summer 2000, pp. 28–29.

Fowler, J. W. *Stages of Faith: The Psychology of Human Development and the Quest for Meaning.* San Francisco: Harper, 1981.

Kuh, G. D., and others. *Involving Colleges: Encouraging Student Learning and Personal Development Through Out-of-Class Experiences.* San Francisco: Jossey-Bass, 1991.

Levinson, D. J., and Levinson, J. D. *The Seasons of a Woman's Life.* New York: Ballantine Books, 1996.

Love, P., and Talbot, D. "Defining Spiritual Development: A Missing Consideration for Student Affairs." *NASPA Journal,* 1999, *37,* 361–375.

McColman, C. *Spirituality: Where Body and Soul Encounter the Sacred.* Georgetown, Mass.: North Star, 1997.

National Association of Student Personnel Administrators. "A Perspective on Student Affairs: A Statement Issued on the 50th Anniversary of the Student Personnel Point of View." Washington, D.C.: NASPA, 1987.

Oldenberg, R. *The Great Good Place.* New York: Paragon House, 1989.

Palmer, P. "Community, Conflict, and Ways of Knowing." *Change,* Sep.–Oct. 1987, 20–25.

Palmer, P. "The Courage to Teach: Exploring the Inner Landscape of a Teacher's Life." San Francisco: Jossey-Bass, 1998.

Palmer, P. "Evoking the Spirit." *Educational Leadership,* Dec. 1998-Jan. 1999, 6–11.

Parks, S. *The Critical Years: Young Adults and the Search for Meaning, Faith, and Commitment.* San Francisco: Harper, 1986.

Parks, S. *Big Questions, Worthy Dreams: Mentoring Young Adults in Their Search for Meaning, Purpose, and Faith.* San Francisco: Jossey-Bass, 2000.

Strange, C. "Spirituality at State: Private Journeys and Public Visions." *Journal of College and Character,* 2000. [http://collegevalues.org/articles.cfm?a=1andid=134]

Strange, C., and Alston, L. "Voicing Differences: Encouraging Multicultural Learning." *Journal of College Student Development,* 1998, *39,* 87–99.

Strange, C., and Banning, J. *Educating by Design: Creating Campus Learning Environments That Work.* San Francisco: Jossey-Bass, 2001.

Young, R. B. *No Neutral Ground: Standing by the Values We Prize in Higher Education.* San Francisco: Jossey-Bass, 1997.

Zohar, D., and Marshall, I. *Connecting with Our Spiritual Intelligence.* New York: Bloomsbury, 2000.

C. CARNEY STRANGE is professor of higher education and student affairs at Bowling Green University, Ohio.

7

A practitioner and faculty member reflects upon her spiritual journey through higher education, drawing on her life experiences and her ethnic background.

Spirit and Nature in Everyday Life: Reflections of a *Mestiza* in Higher Education

Alicia Fedelina Chávez

"Go out and walk by the river and think about life. Consider your place in the world."

Such was the message I often heard from my mother, Josefita Gonzales Chávez, as I was growing up in the mountains of northern New Mexico. These words still resonate through my spirit as I go about my professional life, connecting with students, stewarding a division of student affairs, teaching in a graduate preparation program in college student personnel, and facilitating the continuous multicultural transformation of university operations.

My path in this profession has become increasingly clear as I pay attention to signs around and in me. I am speaking spiritually, of a sense of myself as a whole, authentic, human being living in connection and communion with those around me. This spiritual journey is challenging yet continues to be my most important work. I was raised in a family that is *Mestizo*, a term referring to the multigenerational blending of Spanish and Native American cultures (Anzaldúa, 1987). This blending is so complex that it has taken me years to develop and gain a sense of which of our traditions and beliefs come from each cultural tradition. My spiritual ways of being originate in these cultures and form the foundation of my professional sense of self.

NEW DIRECTIONS FOR STUDENT SERVICES, no. 95, Fall 2001   © John Wiley & Sons, Inc.

Recently, thoughtful scholars and practitioners have been writing about personal and workplace spirituality. Senge and others (1999) describe spirituality as the space, freedom, and safety to bring our whole beings to work. Senge suggests that if spiritual intelligence is absent we become tired, fractured, and dissatisfied. We begin to feel invisible. Thomas (1994) frames this same need in the context of productivity among the many types of difference in our current U.S. workforce. He points out that the culture of the organization must evolve in ways that enable each individual to bring the whole natural self into the workplace. He finds that this creates the maximum potential for each to offer the utmost contribution. Myss (1997) urges us to pay attention to our spirit and intuition as we make choices that affect our health and well being. The Dalai Lama, too, in *Ethics for a New Millennium* (2000), urges a spiritual way of being in every aspect of our lives.

Increasingly, individuals in higher education are identifying the need for more reflective, spiritual practice in our universities. David Scott (Scott and Awbrey, 1993), chancellor at the University of Massachusetts in Amherst, calls for our evolution toward a more integrative definition of knowledge, practice of research, and facilitation of student learning. He points out the need for those of us in higher education not to reject science and objectivity but rather resist relying only on the sciences in contributing to our worldview. "Key to our future," he says, "will be the concept of the complete individual, with a greater sense of wholeness and connectedness.

Education must adopt an integrative philosophy of knowledge, including religion and spirituality, which have been largely eliminated from formal education in public institutions for more than a century." (p. 5). Stephen Gould, in *Rock of Ages: Science and Religion in the Fullness of Life* (1999), urges consideration that "science and religion are needed for true wisdom, since any interesting problem at any scale . . . must call upon the separate contributions of both . . . for any adequate illumination"(p. 65). Parker Palmer (1998) as well often describes teaching as a spiritual endeavor.

Like Palmer, I see my work as vocation, as purpose, and as sacred. While stating my teaching philosophy for my first faculty annual review years ago, I wrote of teaching as a sacred responsibility, tying it to my felt responsibility to serve others. In later considering accepting the position of dean of students at the University of Wisconsin, I listened to an intuitive and spiritual call for me to take up this responsibility, even though I knew it would be a challenging and sometimes painful role. This call was clear even though my heart, mind, and body longed for my New Mexico mountains, my extended family, and continued work as a teacher and scholar offered by another position. Following this spiritual and intuitive voice was clearly a choice. Although I do question it at times, I continue to feel a sacred responsibility to serve others in the context of higher education.

Ironically, little of my spiritual grounding has been shaped by higher education or even by educational environments. This life's foundation has instead been shaped by familial, cultural, reflective, and religious influences in my life. My journey as a spiritual being has its foundations in two primary philosophical traditions. In a religious sense, I was raised in a Spanish Catholic faith and practice. Although I disagree with some principles of Catholicism, some of my deepest values, beliefs, and practice originate in this tradition. In a broader, spiritual sense, Native American precepts have been a foundation of my life through subtle and consistent teachings from my parents, grandparents, and great uncles and aunts. In addition, starting in college, I began to read deeply from other world religions and spiritual traditions, especially from Buddhist philosophy, finding commonality with many Catholic and Native teachings and principles to enrich my spiritual journey.

Over the years, I have become increasingly mindful of developing principles that guide my life. These principles have become clear in my thoughts and practice over time and are, at this point in my life, foundational in my way of being. I have developed them through reflective practice; collaboration with others; listening both to the teaching of those around me and to various spiritual teachings; and by listening to my own inner sense, my own intuition, my own connection to spirit. I catalogue these principles in this way:

Live a reflective life
Practice balance
Embody compassion
Hold relationships as sacred responsibility
Maintain connectedness
Sustain openness
Steward
Radiate hopefulness
Live simply
Give thanks

As I work to facilitate empowering, holistic environments within a university context, I find that no matter how difficult or painful or joyful the work, spirituality moves me toward student affairs practice and scholarship, not as a way of doing but as a way of being. Let me illustrate one higher education context in which I enacted these principles. Each principle discussed is italicized in this example; later in this chapter I provide detailed descriptions of the ten.

While teaching a graduate college student personnel course in group development over a four-year period, I worked to co-construct an authentic, congruent learning experience with each group of students. I invited my fellow learners to join me in creating our own way of being as a community.

As part of my dedication to *maintaining connectedness* with the world around me, and contrary to many faculty cultures, I worked to share authority with students. I facilitated development of shared guides for our work together and ways for us to hold each other accountable.

As part of a sense of *balance,* I challenged students to bring their whole selves to class, and challenged ourselves to facilitate ways to find shared meaning in our learning community. I encouraged students to *hold our relationships sacred* within our learning community and treat each other with a high level of *compassion* and respect.

In bringing their whole selves to class, students became open and vulnerable to learning from each other. Tears, laughter, and even anger were common occurrences in the class as we daily renewed our commitment to stay engaged. I supported this process and students also by *sustaining my own openness* as a learner and in *radiating hopefulness* about our potential as a learning community.

Important in this process was bringing my whole self to class, complete with emotions, personal stories, and candid views. I communicated an expectation that they work with me as a whole human being and not just as "the professor." Together we renamed the course "Building Purposeful Communities in Higher Education," created shared evaluation and grading processes, developed and facilitated the curriculum collectively, and moved purposefully through Scott Peck's stages of community building (1993). Each of us was supported in working toward *reflective,* purposeful student affairs practice and developing skill to facilitate staff and student communities in higher education.

My journey as a spiritual student affairs practitioner and scholar has been one toward living reflectively and in congruence with a set of living principles. I strive toward applying these principles authentically, wholly, and spiritually in my daily professional life. In this chapter, I describe and illustrate each of these principles and discuss how I practice them within the context of university life. In addition, I outline ways in which I encourage others to explore their own journey and to live authentically, as well as discuss the challenge of communities of difference within this context.

Principles of Spiritual Being

In striving to live as an authentic, spiritual being, I am purposeful about living in congruence with a set of principles that I have developed over time. Though doing so will always be something that I need to be mindful about, I find the more these spiritual principles have become my way of being, the easier in many ways it is to be myself and to make choices in my daily practice. I believe this is in great part because I feel free to be the same person in the professional and personal arenas, that I am able to share my full self, and that I continue to take the time regularly to reflect on how I wish to live my life.

Live a Reflective Life. Living reflectively is perhaps the most foundational of all the principles I live by; it affects my ability to live by all of the others. Concepts of contemplative or reflective life originate for me in both Catholicism and Native spiritual teachings. Reflection is critical in my everyday life as it enables me to make conscious choices that are in congruence with my beliefs. Spending time in reflection is encouraged in Catholic teachings. Doing so outside and finding a centering energy in nature are additional messages of Native teachings with which I was raised. I find that in Wisconsin, with its extensive availability of public, protected lands and the beauty of the lake region, I can once again find places to center myself daily and deeply. I regularly use weekends as centering opportunities to walk, camp, and spend large amounts of time outdoors.

In some places I have lived and worked, I found only tiny amounts of public land and experienced great difficulty in finding spiritual renewal. In these places, I experienced a sense of closing in and feeling stifled, as I was unable to connect with the energy of the land around me. As an administrator and teacher in higher education, this reflective time is something I purposefully create with staff and students. I make expectations clear for staff that reflective attention toward one's self is critical to working effectively with students and colleagues as well as in dealing with the complexity of challenges on today's campuses.

In addition, I work with staff to create shared reflective time on our living vision and the processing of issues and needs as they arise. This assists us in developing learning environments and services for students. It also enables us to prepare for the deep work of acting as a catalyst for the transformative evolution necessary in our increasingly diverse institutions of higher education. I encourage staff to schedule time in their week for reflection on their own principles in their daily work, and on long-term solutions.

At first, the challenge is to assist staff and students to learn the value of time spent away from doing to learn to be comfortable with stillness and reflection in their lives. Many student affairs professionals and students we serve need time and assistance to develop this new skill. It may even be frightening for some individuals who are strong external processors or not used to spending time alone with their thoughts. I find this type of discomfort to be fairly common, perhaps because we attract so many external processors and extroverts in student affairs. Students and staff have oftentimes never experienced the positive outcomes of learning from themselves through reflection and benefit from guidance, practice, and reassurance in this area.

Practice Balance. In all things, balance is something Chávez family members are fond of reminding each other about. Balance as a foundational precept is represented in everything, for instance in the circular images of most Native cultural symbols (including the *zia* symbol of balance represented on the New Mexico state flag). This principle of balance involves living in balance with all life forms, and living in healthy ways every day. It encourages consideration of many perspectives and many voices in any decision or action. Balance is something that I have become increasingly purposeful about incorporating into my own professional way. I also encourage others to consider— and even to be held accountable for—balance in their professional practice. This principle connects in a variety of ways to many of our student affairs principles (see the 1937 *Student Personnel Point of View* and ACPA's *Student Learning Imperative*, 1994).

A common philosophical theme in our profession is encouragement to work with students and each other as whole human beings, to consider the wide diversity and many perspectives of individuals in our collegiate communities, and to balance our own urge to serve with our belief that students are adults. Our developmental theories strive to be guides for balancing the student's moral, social, cognitive, and identity development. Learning theories such as Gardner's work on the multiple intelligences (1993) and personality theories such as that of Myers-Briggs and McCaulley (1985) underscore the need to balance the many ways that individuals contribute to and learn from their environments.

Balance is also important in working with staff members as whole people. We need to facilitate bringing our whole authentic self to work and to consider providing for personal needs that staff have, to enable them to contribute productively and effectively. I find that we often understand and accept that students have this requirement but also need to support staff in this area. If I, for instance, have just had a loss in my family, or if I'm ill and cannot process with other staff, I'm probably going to be less patient, less creative, and less able to do complex work effectively.

Time spent together processing, supporting, and developing flexible ways to operate is critical to doing our work well. Among the symptoms of imbalance within a workplace are patterns of illness, burnout, impatience or bursts of emotions, pulling away from others, inappropriate use of vacation or sick leave, and even acts of aggression or abuse of others. As a dean of students, one of my primary messages to students and staff is for them to consider "doing less and doing what we do more deeply and thoughtfully."

As a profession, we have a sacred responsibility to role-model healthy professional behaviors to our students, to take care of other aspects of our lives as well as our work, and to develop ways of working that are effective in the long run, not just the short run. Perhaps most important (taken from words in Christian writings), we should love ourselves as we love our neighbors. Too often, I have seen professionals in our field forget to love themselves in pursuit of caring for those around them. I believe it is essential for each of us to move away from dichotomous ways of being and toward balancing multiple aspects of our life and our work.

Embody Compassion. The philosophies of Mother Teresa and the Dalai Lama have much in common in urging living a life of compassion. While she was alive, Mother Teresa encouraged us to do small things with great love; the Dalai Lama continues to state that his only religion is kindness. Living a life of compassion toward others is the principle that I have taken perhaps most to heart from Catholic scripture and teachings.

Compassion toward myself is one that I have added slowly from Native and Buddhist teachings in my struggle to live healthily and happily in a human service profession. I have learned over time as a student affairs administrator, educator, and scholar to embody compassion as a way of being in my everyday practice. At first it was easy in some aspects of my work and difficult in others. It was easy and natural for me to feel compassionate with students in crisis or with colleagues in need, but less so in judicial hearings or diversity workshops when participants would make hurtful comments.

Some things that have assisted me in truly embodying compassion, even under painful circumstances, are taking time to reflect on my behaviors regularly; working to imagine myself in the place of others; and caring for myself daily so that I have the energy, patience, and emotional peace to work kindly with others. These tools and mindfulness help me maintain a peaceful demeanor even in highly charged situations. I still have times when something comes into my world that jolts me; then I take time to breathe, reflect, and try to understand the situation from the other person's perspective. Even the most hurtful behaviors we see on a college campus always seem to come back to some pain, anger, or frustration that the individuals are coping with prior to their choices.

Working to be tough and kind at the same time are critical to maintaining my compassionate way of being. Once again, it is necessary that we move away from being dichotomous—being either tough or kind. In learning how to be both simultaneously, I am able to work at embodying compassion in my everyday practice.

Hold Relationships as Sacred Responsibility. Highly valuing relationships has clearly originated in familial and cultural teachings in my life. In particular, my father, Gabriel Venceslado Chávez, has sent a consistent and regular message to our family that we must hold relationships as a sacred responsibility. He speaks often of this as something that is without question and without exception, that no matter what, we must return to our relationships and work through conflict or difficulty. I believe this originates in both Spanish and Native clan traditions of spirituality, responsibility, and survival.

I have translated this principle into my professional work by facilitating development and maintenance of strong learning and working communities in higher education; in a constant practice of staying engaged with others regardless of the circumstances; and in my purposeful development, in myself and others, of relational skills. In Peters and Waterman's foundational work *In Search of Excellence* (1982), and Allen and Cherrey's student affairs work *Systemic Leadership* (2000), entire chapters are dedicated to the power of relationships in an organization's success. Roosevelt Thomas, in *Beyond Race and Gender* (1994), discusses the criticality of working through relationships across differences toward task completion for ultimate effectiveness in an organization.

One of the reasons I feel called toward scholarship, teaching, consulting, and activism in the area of diversity and multiculturalism is my sense of purpose in holding relationships sacred as my professional way of being. To do so, especially as a Native and Spanish professional, I work across differences in values, ways of operating, priorities, and perspectives. Because I believe in and thrive on long-term relationships, and because of its effectiveness, I often create an "extended family" in my work environment. We need to articulate purposefully the connection of strong relationships to our primary vision, goals, and objectives. We need to develop relational skills to assist us and those we serve to work effectively across differences to grapple collectively with the increasingly complex issues facing our campuses. We need to dedicate ourselves minute by minute to stay engaged regardless of the circumstances.

Maintain Connectedness. Connectedness is a critical term in many spiritual traditions. It manifests in various forms: the circle of life in numerous Native traditions, the Holy Spirit in Christian traditions, intuition for many nonreligious traditions, spiritual energy forms in the universe in many Eastern belief systems, and what one close friend of mine refers to as listening to "Mother Universe." Maintaining connectedness in my everyday life means I need constantly to listen to more than my five senses. Raised with a mixture of Native traditions, I find it essential to connect with this spirit or energy through time spent out in nature's vibrant places. I find myself in great spiritual distress when I lack the opportunity for time spent at least weekly in parks, forests, or mountains.

My most critical guide in making life choices is my spirit or intuition. I have learned—sometimes the hard way—that even when my heart, mind, and body point in one direction, I need to listen and follow what my intuition and spirit quietly call me to do. At times this has meant going in a direction that at first makes little logical sense, or one toward which others around me are skeptical. After a time, the rightness of my choice has always become clear.

I also have become purposeful in encouraging students and professionals to listen to and learn from all parts of themselves, including their own intuition or spirit. At first, this feels like a great risk for me, to openly encourage intuition and not rationality in the academy. Whenever group members in workshops I facilitate share one aspect of themselves that does not feel welcome in higher education, many express that their spiritual self feels unwelcome and unacknowledged. As I have become purposeful about this, however, lines of people form to relay some story and to share that I am the first one who has ever encouraged them to consider this quiet-but-present guide in their public lives. This connectedness for me is not just an individual source. It is as well a place for us to consider shared spirit and to support each other with this connectedness.

Sustain Openness. The principle that attracts me perhaps most strongly to working in an educational environment is sustaining openness in my life. This points me toward lifelong learning, another connection to our profession. Being open enables me to consider multiple perspectives and to surround myself with others who embody and practice those perspectives. I believe this is the hallmark of a true learning community. We need to create environments empowering of multiple ideas, ways of knowing, ways of learning, and ways of contributing. A very wise supervisor, Gary Schwartz, in the department of residence at Iowa State University, once urged us hall directors to select at least a few staff who made us actively uncomfortable, to create a truly diverse staff team. I have never forgotten this message and have since developed my ability to determine the difference between discomfort that is a legitimate intuitive warning from discomfort that signals a need for me to work across positive differences.

Richard Quantz, a former colleague in my faculty department at Miami University, reminded me at one point that even those with beliefs far from our own are likely trying just as hard as we are to live by what they believe is right and good. Over time, I have become most comfortable in working professionally in highly diverse groups because of the level of creativity, the multiple types of spirit, and the marvelous possibilities. Being an educator for me is based in large part on my way of being as a person who sustains openness, values a multiplicity of perspectives, and encourages them in others.

Steward. Stewardship is a principle of living a purposeful life and working to make a difference in the world. Wilma Mankiller, chief of the Cherokee nation, often speaks of our shared responsibility for "seven generations into the future," not just for humans but for other beings and for the earth that is our home. Stewardship means living a purposeful life; it is part of a definition of a well-lived life within many Native and Spanish contexts. A life with an individual career as the center is often seen as too individualistic and even as inappropriate or selfish. In many collective cultures and spiritual traditions, living a life of purpose is a guiding principle; stewardship is a way in which one might do this.

I have made a variety of transitions in our profession within student affairs, as a diversity consultant and educator, and as a faculty member teaching and doing scholarship in educational administration. With each of these transitions, I have made choices primarily based on how I feel called to stewardship. I consistently feel that my role in the world is to be an interpreter and facilitator among many ways of being, and that educational environments are where I can have an important influence. In my most recent transition, my personal longings for home, family, and the mountains of New Mexico gave way to a strong spiritual and intuitive sense that I needed to be at the University of Wisconsin, Madison. My life's purpose continues to guide me in my professional and personal choices.

Radiate Hopefulness. Some of the most important aspects of my professional practice are wrapped up in my personal principle of radiating hopefulness. Students and professionals seem to bring to campus increasing feelings of loneliness and hopelessness about their life. Changing societal parameters, movement of many families toward distant locations, the astounding influx of information bombardment, multiple choices available for almost everything, and an emphasis on consumerism may be contributing factors. I work to assist others to see the incredible worth in their own spirit, talent, and contributions—to see, in the words of developmental theorist Roy Heath, "all the marvelous possibilities" of the human spirit (1964, p. 75).

When identifying challenges, I offer hope for creating solutions in the form of ideas and suggestions, and by calling people together to develop a multitude of possible strategies. It is imperative for me to assist staff and students in searching for the best in each other and believing in our ability to continue improving. Reminding staff to give others the benefit of the doubt and to work at learning the reasons behind each other's choices is a small but critical way in which we can keep hope alive in our own professional communities. It is critical as well for me to facilitate joy, fun, and opportunity for celebration in our everyday work.

Live Simply. The principle of living simply has its origins in many spiritual traditions in my life. From Native traditions, simplicity enables me to focus on what is important, to listen to the universe around me; it is a way of honoring my place in a world shared with other beings. In both Buddhism and Catholicism, simplicity is a virtue that enables us to clear our minds of distraction and the pull of things we do not consider important in the long run. In professional practice, I encourage simplicity in our work by facilitating a staff focus on solutions closest to the challenge; by promoting realistic, long-term choices about use of resources; and by encouraging staff to do a few things and do them deeply. Considering more than the human element in all that we do and facilitating a wide ethic in our use of resources, buildings, and grounds in higher education assists me personally and professionally.

Give Thanks. A practice of giving thanks is foundational in so many spiritual traditions and important in our own profession as well. We have so much to be thankful for in our privileged work in higher education: the marvelous spirit of our students, the kindness of our colleagues, the excitement of working in an environment of constant learning, and the joy of doing work that makes a difference in the lives of others.

Some of my most important work is the small daily practice of letting others know how much I value and benefit from their presence, their wisdom, and their contributions. When people feel good about themselves, I find that they are also likely to be patient with others, try to understand different perspectives, and develop creative, long-term solutions to complex issues. I find it is also helpful to continuously place our work in the context of a larger world and to remind ourselves of all the blessings we have in our profession.

Final Words

In closing, I would like to share once again the words of an important leader in our society, Chief Wilma Mankiller. I find it helpful to purposefully develop and be mindful of my own principles daily; I encourage you to reflect on the practice of your own principles in your chosen vocation. I wish you well on your journey as you continue to reflect and develop an increased sense of who you are and how you live your spiritual beliefs in professional practice. "We must live life," Wilma says, "as full, authentic, human beings . . . living honorably and sharing responsibility for seven generations into the future."

References

Allen, K., and Cherrey, C. *Systemic Leadership: Enriching the Meaning of Our Work*. Lanham, Md.: University Press of America, 2000.

American College Personnel Association. *The Student Learning Imperative: Implications for Student Affairs*. Alexandria, Va.: ACPA, 1994.

American Council on Education. "The Student Personnel Point of View." In A. L. Rentz (ed.), *Student Affairs: A Profession's Heritage*. (American College Personnel Association Media Publication, no. 40, 2nd ed.) Lanham, Md.: University Press of America, 1994. (Original work published in 1937)

Anzaldúa, G. *Borderlands/La Frontera: The New Mestiza*. San Francisco: Ant Lute Books, 1987.

Dalai Lama. *Ethics for a New Millennium*. New York: River Head Books, 2000.

Gardner, H. *Frames of Mind: The Theory of Multiple Intelligences*. Boston: Basic Books, 1993.

Gould, S. *Rock of Ages: Science and Religion in the Fullness of Life*. London: Ballantine, 1999.

Heath, R. *The Reasonable Adventurer: A Study of the Development of Thirty-Six Undergraduates at Princeton*. Pittsburgh: Pittsburgh Press, 1964.

Myers-Briggs, I., and McCaulley, M. H. *Manual: A Guide to the Development and Use of Myers-Briggs Type Indicator*. Palo Alto, Calif.: Consulting Psychologists Press, 1985.

Myss, S. *Anatomy of the Spirit: Seven Stages of Power and Healing*. New York: Random House, 1997.

Palmer, P. *The Courage to Teach: Exploring the Inner Landscape of a Teacher's Life*. San Francisco: Jossey-Bass, 1998.

Peck, S. "Stages of Community Building." In C. Whitmyer (ed.), *In the Company of Others: Making Community in the Modern World*. New York: Putnam, 1993.

Peters, T., and Waterman, R. *In Search of Excellence: Lessons from America's Best-Run Companies*. New York: Warner, 1982.

Scott, D., and Awbrey, S. "Transforming the University." Paper presented at the Conference on Women in Science and Engineering, Bloomington, Ind., 1993.

Senge, P., and others. *The Dance of Change*. New York: Doubleday, 1999.

Thomas, R. *Beyond Race and Gender: Managing Your Total Workforce*. New York: AMACOM, 1994.

Wheatley, M. *Leadership and the New Science: Learning About Organizations from an Orderly Universe*. San Francisco: Berrett-Koehler, 1992.

ALICIA FEDELINA CHÁVEZ *is the dean of students at the University of Wisconsin, Madison, and has an adjunct appointment in the School of Education.*

8

Books, retreat centers, Websites, and other resources are provided for further exploration.

Annotated References

Shirley Williams

The purpose of this list is to help the interested reader start exploring spiritual development. It is far from comprehensive. Included are sites that allow the curious the opportunity to explore from a number of faith traditions and perspectives. Enjoy! Peace!

Books

The Bhagavad Gita

The Holy Bible

The Koran

The Torah

Armstrong, K. *A History of God: A 4,000-Year Quest of Judaism, Christianity, and Islam.* New York: Ballantine Books, 1993.
  Traces the history of how humankind has understood God and how the three major monotheistic religions are connected through history.

Bach, R. *Jonathan Livingston Seagull.* New York: Avon Books, 1970.
  The metaphorical story of a seagull who dared to challenge the teachings of the flock in order that he might strive to reach perfect flight.

Bowman, L. G., and Deal, T. E. *Leading with Soul: An Uncommon Journey of Spirit.* San Francisco: Jossey-Bass, 1995.
    Using the timeless art of storytelling to instruct, the authors tell the story of a leader's quest to find leadership and how, in the process, he finds his soul.

Buber, M. *I and Thou.* (R. G. Smith, trans.) New York: Macmillan, 1958.
    This classic provides mystical insight into theological and interpersonal relationships from both Jewish and Christian traditions.

Carter, F. *The Education of Little Tree.* Albuquerque: University of New Mexico Press, 1976.
    Follow the life of a young Cherokee boy, raised by his grandparents immersed in native traditions. Witness his clash with white culture as he is forced into white "Indian schools" and his ultimate rejoining of his native home.

Parks, L.A.P., Keen, C. H., Keen, J. P., and Parks, S. D. *Common Fire: Leading Lives of Commitment in a Complex World.* Boston, Mass.: Beacon Press, 1996.
    Helps the reader understand what it means to live a life of commitment, the traits and characteristics that reinforce one's life of serving others.

De Pree, M. *Leading Without Power: Finding Hope in Serving Community.* San Francisco: Jossey-Bass, 1997.
    This well-known leadership author offers a new paradigm for leading, doing so from the perspective of serving the organization and its members. This shift in focus offers those who embrace it a new empowerment based on giving power rather than grabbing it.

Estes, C. P. *The Faithful Gardener.* San Francisco: Harper, 1995.
    Follow the stories of the author's uncle, witnessing the power of faithfulness in one's life and commitments, which supports and sustains in times of change and turmoil.

Gellman, M., and Hartman, T. *How Do You Spell God?* New York: Morrow Junior Books, 1995.
    "The God Squad" provides insights into the major religions using humor and sincere appreciation of the differences and similarities.

Gibran, K. *The Prophet.* New York: Alfred A. Knopf, 1985. (Originally published in 1923)
    A classic. Treat yourself to this mystic's insights into important life-and-death questions.

Greenleaf, R. K. *Servant Leadership: A Journey into the Nature of Legitimate Power and Greatness.* New York: Paulist Press, 1977.

This pioneer of the servant leadership movement introduces the reader to servant leadership and applies the concept throughout all of our major institutions.

Hanh, T. N. *Living Buddha, Living Christ.* New York: Berkley, 1995.
An insightful and deeply spiritual journey into Christian and Buddhist theology and the impact on the world. A real ecumenical treasure.

Heifetz, R. A. *Leadership Without Easy Answers.* Cambridge, Mass.: Belknap, 1994.
Essential reading for anyone in a leadership position. By using real examples of some of the best known leaders in recent history, Heifetz offers useful suggestions of approaching leadership in a way that maintains integrity.

Hillman, J. *The Soul's Code: In Search of Character and Calling.* New York: Warner Books, 1996.
This well-known author offers new empowerment to our personal choices, giving the soul the strength and ability to assert itself in showing its true nature. This insight can then be used to inform the many life decisions facing us.

Millman, D. *Way of the Peaceful Warrior.* Tiburon, Calif.: H. J. Kramer, 1980.
Follow the author's journey into self-exploration and discovery, led by his guide, Socrates. This journey teaches Millman the life of a Peaceful Warrior.

Millman, D. *Sacred Journey of the Peaceful Warrior.* Tiburon, Calif.: H. J. Kramer, 1991.
A continuation of Millman's spiritual quest, reminding us that it is the journey that is the point of the quest.

Moore, T. *Care of the Soul: A Guide for Cultivating Depth and Sacredness in Everyday Life.* New York: Harper Perennial, 1992.
Deeply insightful writing on caring for and honoring the wisdom of the soul as we live our lives and strive to grow as spiritual beings.

Morgan, M. *Mutant Message Down Under.* New York: Harper Perennial, 1991.
Aboriginal tribal wisdom is shared with an American woman as she makes a fourteen-hundred-mile, four-month trek in the Outback. Deeply moving in its spiritual lessons.

Peck, M. S. *The Road Less Traveled.* New York: Simon & Schuster, 1978.
Combining spiritual and psychological insights, *The Road Less Traveled* offers definitions and approaches to conflict, love, grace, and other life experiences.

Redfield, J. *The Celestine Prophesy.* New York: Warner, 1993.

A parable that gripped the nation just seven years ago. Offers insights into spiritual truths of humanity.

Silverstein, S. *The Giving Tree.* New York: HarperCollins, 1964.

A parable of giving and loving unconditionally, and recognizing in others the limited capacity of understanding those gifts.

Sims, B. J. *Servanthood: Leadership for the Third Millennium.* Cambridge, Mass.: Cowley, 1997.

Bishop Sims, retired from the Episcopal church and a colleague of Robert Greenleaf's, takes the servant-leadership model and applies it to the church. Challenges church leaders to reexamine their understanding of leadership.

Smith, H. *The Illustrated World Religions: A Guide to Our Wisdom Traditions.* San Francisco: Harper, 1994.

Renowned author gives a basic overview of the major religions of the world. Wonderful resource for college campuses.

Whyte, D. *The Heart Aroused: Poetry and the Preservation of the Soul in the Workplace.* New York: Currency/Doubleday, 1994.

Using poetry, mythology, and personal experience, the author challenges the corporate world to open itself to the souls of its employees, offering the organization the possibility of integrated staff who practice courageous speech and serve with integrity.

Spiritual Retreat Websites

http://www.kripalushop.org/kripalu/

Website of Kripalu, the largest center for yoga and holistic health in the United States, serving people of all backgrounds. Offers a large number of experiential yoga, self-discovery, holistic health, and spiritual programs that present ancient yogic principles in a contemporary way.

http://personalretreat.com/

This site gives tips on how to conduct one's own spiritual retreat, including readings, fasting, and creating the appropriate space.

http://amritherapy.com/otherretreats.htm

This site lists a number of retreat centers across the United States that offer a range of services.

http://www.spiritsite.com/centers/index.htm

Although not comprehensive, this site offers the visitor a considerable listing of spiritual retreat centers supporting a range of interests. Sites are listed geographically. Other resources for finding spiritual retreat centers are included.

http://www.lectiodivina.org/retreats.htm

This site offers a listing of retreat centers from around the world where the focus is contemplative prayer.

http://www.maitrhea.org/retreatcenter.html

Although not comprehensive, this site offers the visitor a listing of spiritual retreat centers supporting a range of interests and open to varying traditions. Sites are listed geographically.

http://www.manitou.org/mf_spiritual_ctrs.html

A resource of religious centers and spiritual projects in the region of Crestone/Baca, Colorado. Includes a Catholic monastery, Zen and Tibetan Buddhist centers, a Hindu ashram, and others.

http://www.osb.org/retreats/index.html

A listing of Association of Benedictine Retreat Centers across Canada and the United States.

http://dioceseofstpete.org/retreat_centers_used_by_the_dioc.htm

A listing of retreat centers used by the Roman Catholic Diocese of St. Petersburg.

http://www.metrogate.com/scrapce/page2.html

A listing of retreat centers affiliated with the Presbyterian church and located in the central and southwestern parts of the United States.

http://www.groupmag.com/pcrc.htm

Listing of pastoral care retreat centers across the United States. Focuses on those who provide pastoral care for others, both clergy and lay ministry.

http://www.greenho.com/Home_Page/home_page.html

The Greenhouse Art and Retreat Center, dedicated to the artist in everyone.

http://www.fivemtn.org/health/spas.html

Spas and retreat centers in Hawaii. Offers a range of experiences and faith and spiritual backgrounds.

http://www.wju.edu/jesuits/centers.html

A listing of Jesuit retreat houses and renewal centers in the United States.

http://www.vaumc.org/Retreat/retreat.htm

Retreat Centers for the United Methodist church located across the United States.

http://www.diamondway-buddhism.org/kkbn-cen.htm
A worldwide listing of more than 270 Buddhist centers and retreat centers of the Karma Kagyu lineage. Listed by country.

http://www.womenspress.com/directory/retreats.html
The Minnesota Women's Press business and resource guide to retreats and retreat centers.

http://www.allaboutretreats.com/canada.html
A listing of retreat centers in the United States, Canada, Mexico, and Costa Rica.

http://llamalinks.com/retreat1.html
A listing of spiritual retreat sites, including spas and a range of spiritual traditions.

http://naturalhealthweb.com/topics/subtopics/retreats_&_retreat_centers.html
A listing of spiritual retreat centers published by NaturalHealth.com. Located in sites around the world.

Interfaith Resource Websites

http://www.spiritualsearch.net/
The site for the Spiritual Search Engine, a comprehensive site offering information on all of the major religions as well as specific topic areas, such as spiritual practice, books, health and healing, food, and so on.

http://www.ashram.com/
An online resource for retreat centers; health and wellness information in the yoga tradition; and shopping for books, videos, music, and natural apparel.

http://www.urantiabook.org/interfaith_links.htm
This site includes academic and scholarly research, directories, interfaith organizations, articles, and online religious text.

http://linking-library.virtualave.net/dir/rel.html
Vast resource for searching on a range of faith traditions and topic areas. Also includes other search engine information on the topic of religion.

http://www.martinrutte.com/groups.html
A list of spirituality-in-the-workplace resources, both speakers and groups, where one can network or order products.

http://www.wellesley.edu/RelLife/transformation/main.htm
Education as Transformation Project home page, Wellesley College. Its purpose is to initiate dialogue about religious pluralism and spirituality in

higher education. Sponsored a national conference and is continuing its work in publishing articles and books on related topics.

http://csf.colorado.edu/sine/index.html
The Website for the Spirituality in Education Conference, sponsored by Naropa Institute. Includes conference proceedings and selected conference transcripts.

http://www.interfaithcalendar.org/
A resource for the primary sacred dates and times in world religions; also includes definitions, links, book resources, and so forth.

Miscellaneous Resources

http://www.21learn.org/arch/articles/palmer_spirituality.html
Palmer, P. "The Violence of our Knowledge: Toward a Spirituality of Higher Education." Michael Keenan Memorial Lecture, Berea College, Ky., seventh lecture, 1993.

http://www.collegeandcharacter.org/guide/resource.html
College and Character: A National Initiative of the John Templeton Foundation. This resource directory profiles seventy higher education organizations that encourage—through programs or publications—one or more dimensions of character development.

http://jaie.asu.edu/v30/V30S3fir.htm
Kirkness, V. J., and Barnhardt, R. "First Nations and Higher Education: The Four Rs—Respect, Relevance, Reciprocity, Responsibility." *Journal of American Indian Education.*

http://www.uic.edu/depts/quic/oglbc/resources/religion.html
Website for books on religion and spirituality focusing on the gay, lesbian, bisexual, transgender community.

http://www.buddhanet.net
Buddhist Information Network.

http://www.bahai.org/
Web page introducing the Bahai faith.

SHIRLEY WILLIAMS *is the assistant dean of students at the University of New England, Biddeford, Maine, and is working on a divinity degree at Harvard University.*

Index

SINGLE ISSUE SALE

For a limited time save 10% on single issues! Save an additional 10% when you purchase three or more single issues. Each issue is normally 27\frac{00}{}$.

Please see the next page for a complete listing of available back issues.

Mail or fax this completed form to: Jossey-Bass, A Wiley Company
989 Market Street • San Francisco CA 94103-1741

CALL OR FAX

Phone 888-378-2537 or 415-433-1740 *or Fax* 800-605-2665 or 415-433-4611 (*attn customer service*)
BE SURE TO USE PROMOTION CODE ND2 TO GUARANTEE YOUR DISCOUNT!
Please send me the following issues at 24\frac{30}{}$ each.

(Important: please include series initials and issue number, such as SS94)

1. SS _____

_____

_____

$ _____ Total for single issues (25\frac{20}{}$ each)

_____ Less 10% if ordering 3 or more issues

_____ Shipping charges: Up to $30, add 5\frac{50}{}$ • 30\frac{01}{}$ –$50, add 6\frac{50}{}$ 50\frac{01}{}$ –$75, add 7\frac{50}{}$ • 75\frac{01}{}$ –$100, add 9\frac{00}{}$ • 100\frac{01}{}$ –$150, add 10\frac{00}{}$
Over $150, call for shipping charge

$ _____ Total (Add appropriate sales tax for your state. Canadian residents add GST)

❑ Payment enclosed (U.S. check or money order only)
❑ VISA, MC, AmEx Discover Card # _____ Exp. date _____
Signature _____
Day phone _____
❑ Bill me (U.S. institutional orders only. Purchase order required)
Purchase order # _____
    Federal Tax ID. 135593032   GST 89102 8052
Name _____
Address _____

_____

Phone _____ E-mail _____
For more information about Jossey-Bass, visit our website at: www.josseybass.com

OFFER EXPIRES FEBRUARY 28, 2002.   PRIORITY CODE = ND2

Save Now on the Best of ABOUT CAMPUS Series Sets Enriching the Student Learning Experience

Dedicated to the idea that student learning is the responsibility of all educators on campus, **About Campus** illuminates critical issues faced by both student affairs and academic affairs staff as they work on the shared goal that brought them to the same campus in the first place: to help students learn.

With each issue, **About Campus** combines the imagination and creativity found in the best magazines and the authority and thoughtfulness found in the best professional journals. Now we've taken the four most popular issues from three volume years and we've made them available as a set— at a tremendous savings over our $20.00 single issue price.

Best of About Campus – Volume 3

Facts and Myths About Assessment in Student Affairs – Why Learning Communities? Why Now? – The Stressed Student: How Can We Help? – Being All That We Can Be
ISBN 0–7879–6128–0 $12.00

Best of About Campus – Volume 4

Increasing Expectations for Student Effort – The Matthew Shepard Tragedy: Crisis and Beyond – Civic and Moral Learning – Faculty-Student Affairs Collaboration on Assessment.
ISBN 0–7879–6129–9 $12.00

Best of About Campus – Volume 5

The Diversity Within – What Can We Do About Student Cheating – Bonfire: Tragedy and Tradition – Hogwarts: The Learning Community.
ISBN 0–7879–6130–2 $12.00

To order by phone: call 1–800–956–7739 or 415–433–1740

Visit our website at www.josseybass.com

Use promotion code **ND2** to guarantee your savings.
Shipping and applicable taxes will be added.

ABOUT CAMPUS

Sponsored by the *American College Personnel Association*
Published by Jossey-Bass, A Wiley Company

Patricia M. King, Executive Editor
Jon C. Dalton, Senior Editor

Published bimonthly. Individual subscriptions $53.00. Institutional subscriptions $95.00.

Jossey-Bass, A Wiley Company • 989 Market St., Fifth Floor • San Francisco, CA 94103–1741

SS90 **Powerful Programming for Student Learning: Approaches That Make a Difference**
Debora L. Liddell, Jon P. Lund
Assists student affairs professionals as they plan, implement, and evaluate their educational interventions on college and university campuses. Details each step of program assessment, planning, implementation, and outcome evaluation. Explains the importance of collaborating with faculty and others, illustrating several types of programming partnerships with four brief case studies and examines the significant partnership aspects that led to programming success. Also examines two of today's most relevant programming topics—multicultural competence and sexual violence—and provides an overview of a number of promising programs covering such areas as service learning, leadership, community-building, alcohol awareness, and diversity.

SS89 **The Role Student Aid Plays in Enrollment Management**
Michael D. Coomes
Explains the often-conflicting relationship between student aid and enrollment management. Examines the political and cultural contexts that influence decisions about student aid and enrollment management, the special enrollment management challenges facing independent colleges, and some alternative methods for financing a college education. Provides a review of the research on the impact of student aid on recruitment and retention, recommendations for ethical enrollment planning, and a list of resources for enrollment planners, researchers, and policymakers.

SS88 **Understanding and Applying Cognitive Development Theory**
Patrick G. Love, Victoria L. Guthrie
Reviews five theories of the cognitive development of college students and explores the applications of those theories to student affairs practice. These theories shed light on gender-related patterns of knowing and reasoning; interpersonal, cultural, and emotional influences on cognitive development; and people's methods of approaching complex issues and defending what they believe.

SS87 **Creating Successful Partnerships Between Academic and Student Affairs**
John H. Schuh, Elizabeth J. Whitt
Presents case studies of academic and student affairs partnerships that have been successfully put into practice at a variety of institutions, in areas such as service learning, the core curriculum, and residential learning communities. Offers practical strategies for forming collaborations that enhance learning and promote student success, and a set of guiding principles to use in assessing the effectiveness of partnerships and the climate for collaboration at individual institutions.

SS86 **Beyond Borders: How International Developments Are Changing International Affairs Practice**
Jon C. Dalton
Assesses the impact of international trends and developments on the student affairs profession, and offers practical suggestions for developing the knowledge and skills requisite for a global future. Explains how to recruit and support international students and provide valuable information on student and staff exchange programs. Presents case studies from student affairs professionals in Mexico, Germany, and Hong Kong, highlighting the global student affairs issues that transcend national borders.

SS85   **Student Affairs Research, Evaluation, and Assessment: Structure and Practice in an Era of Change**
Gary D. Malaney
Illustrates how research can enhance and support the work of the student services staff and the campus at-large. Describes how student affairs and faculty can collaborate to create an agenda for student-related research; reviews technological aids for collecting and analyzing data; and discusses how student affairs researchers can make their role more vital to the campus by expanding into policy analysis and information brokering.

SS84   **Strategies for Staff Development: Personal and Professional Education in the 21st Century**
William A. Bryan, Robert A. Schwartz
Offers a range of strategies for recruiting, retaining, and developing an educated, energetic, and motivated student affairs staff. Examines a performance-based approach to human resource development, the impact of supervisors and mentors on those entering and advancing in the field, and the influence of behavioral style on professional development.

SS83   **Responding to the New Affirmative Action Climate**
Donald D. Gehring
Explores how to achieve an economically, ethnically, spiritually, and culturally diverse student body while complying with confusing and sometimes conflicting laws and judicial pronouncements. Clarifies the law as it relates to affirmative action in admissions and financial aid; discusses alternatives to race-based methods for achieving diversity; and reports on a national study of student affairs programs that have successfully used affirmative action.

SS82   **Beyond Law and Policy: Reaffirming the Role of Student Affairs**
Diane L. Cooper, James M. Lancaster
Examines higher education's apparent overreliance on policy and shows how we can redirect our attention to the ethical and developmental issues that underlie the undergraduate experience. Discusses how learning communities and creeds can help achieve balance between policy and personal responsibility, how to deal with student misconduct in a way that both reduces the risk of litigation and furthers student development, and how to promote multiculturalism without compromising individual rights and freedoms.

SS80   **Helping African American Men Succeed in College**
Michael J. Cuyjet
Offers practical strategies, proven models and programs, and the essential theoretical grounding necessary for nurturing and retaining African American male students. Explores ways to make classroom environments more supportive, the benefits of mentoring initiatives, the opportunities for leadership development on a predominantly white campus, and more.

SS79   **Serving Students at Metropolitan Universities: The Unique Opportunities and Challenges**
Larry H. Dietz, Vicky L. Triponey
Identifies and explores the special challenges and unique opportunities faced by student affairs at metropolitan universities—revealing how to build on the urban setting and the rich diversity of the student population to enhance

student life. Discusses how to develop productive partnerships with the community, the role student affairs can play in institutional planning, and how to budget for critical yet limited resources.

SS78　**Using Technology to Promote Student Learning: Opportunities for Today and Tomorrow**
Catherine McHugh Engstrom, Kevin W. Kruger
Explores critical issues that have developed with the increased use of technology, including strategic planning process needs, financial and infrastructure issues, policy implications, curricular issues for student affairs graduate programs, and ethical considerations.

SS76　**Total Quality Management: Applying Its Principles to Student Affairs**
William A. Bryan
Provides balanced coverage of information for student affairs professionals regarding total quality management (TQM) principles and discusses issues surrounding their use. Provides examples of the application of TQM principles and techniques in student affairs settings.

SS74　**Leveling the Playing Field: Promoting Academic Success for Students of Color**
Irene Harris Johnson, Allen J. Ottens
Provides ideas, narratives, and learning that have relevance for the retention of all students of color but that can be particularly applied to the retention of regularly admitted students of color.

SS73　**Critical Issues in Judicial Affairs**
Wanda L. Mercer
Provides judicial administrators with practical information and guidelines in many aspects of student discipline. Also discusses current trends and recent topics of interest in judicial affairs.

SS72　**Student Services for the Changing Graduate Student Population**
Anne S. Pruitt-Logan, Paul D. Isaac
Discusses support system issues and needs from the points of view of both graduate education and student affairs. Offers excerpts from a graduate student's diary and reviews the current landscape of graduate education.

SS71　**Making Enrollment Management Work**
Rebecca R. Dixon
Examines important areas of enrollment management for the benefit of student service administrators, including the need to integrate a number of activities and programs to find, enroll, and retain enough of the kinds of students an institution wants.

SS70　**Budgeting as a Tool for Policy in Student Affairs**
Dudley B. Woodard, Jr.
Focuses on budgeting as a policy tool for restructuring. Explores the perspective of the changing conditions in higher education, that is, moving beyond cost containment through reductions and combinations toward accountability and effectiveness through restructuring.

SS69   **Promoting Student Success in the Community College**
        Steven R. Helfgot, Marguerite McGann Culp
        Examines the dynamics of change that characterize community college
        students and offers a theoretical base from which to understand today's new
        student. Explores the impact that organizational structure and partnerships
        have on program effectiveness.

SS67   **Successful Drug and Alcohol Prevention Programs**
        Eileen V. Coughlin
        Details the problems of alcohol abuse and other drug use in higher
        education and suggests approaches for creating a campus climate that is
        more conducive to successful social and academic development.

SS57   **Effective AIDS Education on Campus**
        Richard P. Keeling
        Offers analysis, rationale, justification, and guidelines for focusing,
        evaluating, and improving HIV education and sexual health-promotion
        programs on college and university campuses.